Marijuana

Lydia D. Bjornlund

Drugs

ReferencePoint
Press®

San Diego, CA

About the Author

Lydia D. Bjornlund is a freelance writer. She has written almost two dozen nonfiction books for children and teens, mostly on American history and health-related topics. She also writes books and training materials for adults on issues related to conservation and public management, as well as educational testing and curriculum materials. Bjornlund holds a master's degree in education from Harvard University and a BA in American studies from Williams College. She lives in Northern Virginia with her husband, Gerry Hoetmer, and their children, Jake and Sophia.

© 2012 ReferencePoint Press, Inc.
Printed in the United States

For more information, contact:
ReferencePoint Press, Inc.
PO Box 27779
San Diego, CA 92198
www.ReferencePointPress.com

Picture credits:
Cover: iStockphoto.com
Maury Aaseng: 32–34, 47–48, 62–64, 77–79
Thinkstock/iStockphoto: 9, 16

LIBRARY OF CONGRESS CATALOGING-IN-PUBLICATION DATA

Bjornlund, Lydia D.
  Marijuana / by Lydia Bjornlund.
    p. cm.—(Compact research series)
  Includes bibliographical references and index.
  ISBN-13: 978-1-60152-160-6 (hardback)
  ISBN-10: 1-60152-160-X (hardback)
  1. Marijuana—United States—Juvenile literature. 2. Marijuana—Law and legislation—United States—Juvenile literature. I. Title.
  HV5822.M3B47   2012
  362.29'50973—dc22
                                                                        2011007743

YA

Contents

Foreword   4

Marijuana at a Glance   6

Overview   8

Is Marijuana a Dangerous Drug?   19
    Primary Source Quotes   27
    Facts and Illustrations   31

Should Marijuana Be Legal for Medical Use?   35
    Primary Source Quotes   43
    Facts and Illustrations   46

Should Marijuana Be a Legal Substance?   50
    Primary Source Quotes   58
    Facts and Illustrations   61

How Effective Are Efforts to Prevent
    Marijuana Use?   65
    Primary Source Quotes   73
    Facts and Illustrations   76

Key People and Advocacy Groups   80

Chronology   82

Related Organizations   84

For Further Research   88

Source Notes   90

List of Illustrations   92

Index   93

Foreword

"Where is the knowledge we have lost in information?"

—T.S. Eliot, "The Rock."

As modern civilization continues to evolve, its ability to create, store, distribute, and access information expands exponentially. The explosion of information from all media continues to increase at a phenomenal rate. By 2020 some experts predict the worldwide information base will double every 73 days. While access to diverse sources of information and perspectives is paramount to any democratic society, information alone cannot help people gain knowledge and understanding. Information must be organized and presented clearly and succinctly in order to be understood. The challenge in the digital age becomes not the creation of information, but how best to sort, organize, enhance, and present information.

ReferencePoint Press developed the *Compact Research* series with this challenge of the information age in mind. More than any other subject area today, researching current issues can yield vast, diverse, and unqualified information that can be intimidating and overwhelming for even the most advanced and motivated researcher. The *Compact Research* series offers a compact, relevant, intelligent, and conveniently organized collection of information covering a variety of current topics ranging from illegal immigration and deforestation to diseases such as anorexia and meningitis.

The series focuses on three types of information: objective single-author narratives, opinion-based primary source quotations, and facts and statistics. The clearly written objective narratives provide context and reliable background information. Primary source quotes are carefully selected and cited, exposing the reader to differing points of view. And facts and statistics sections aid the reader in evaluating perspectives. Presenting these key types of information creates a richer, more balanced learning experience.

For better understanding and convenience, the series enhances information by organizing it into narrower topics and adding design features that make it easy for a reader to identify desired content. For example, in *Compact Research: Illegal Immigration*, a chapter covering the economic impact of illegal immigration has an objective narrative explaining the various ways the economy is impacted, a balanced section of numerous primary source quotes on the topic, followed by facts and full-color illustrations to encourage evaluation of contrasting perspectives.

The ancient Roman philosopher Lucius Annaeus Seneca wrote, "It is quality rather than quantity that matters." More than just a collection of content, the *Compact Research* series is simply committed to creating, finding, organizing, and presenting the most relevant and appropriate amount of information on a current topic in a user-friendly style that invites, intrigues, and fosters understanding.

Marijuana at a Glance

Prevalence in the United States

According to the 2010 National Survey on Drug Use and Health, roughly 11.3 percent of Americans have used marijuana in the past year and more than 40 percent have used the drug in their lifetimes.

Public Perceptions

Marijuana is viewed by many as far less dangerous than alcohol or some other drugs, while others believe that marijuana's health hazards and other negative impacts have been grossly underestimated.

Effects on the Body

Marijuana gives users a mild feeling of euphoria, but the relaxed high sometimes gives way to anxiety and paranoia. Marijuana also interferes with memory and coordination.

Marijuana Potency

Growers have learned to cultivate increasingly powerful strains of marijuana. One of the more potent strains available—skunk or skunk weed—may be as much as 10 times stronger than the marijuana available in the 1960s.

Concerns About Addiction

For many years experts believed that marijuana was not addictive but recent research suggests otherwise. Longtime marijuana users can find it difficult to quit without help from medical professionals.

Medical Applications

Experts disagree widely on the medical benefits of marijuana, which is most commonly used for pain relief, prevention and treatment of nausea, and treating depression and anxiety.

Legalization

Marijuana is illegal under federal law but 15 states have legalized marijuana for medical purposes. More than three-quarters of Americans believe that marijuana should be legalized for medical use and a growing number appear to favor legalizing marijuana for recreational use as well.

Risks

Marijuana is a primary factor in nearly 374,000 emergency room visits in the United States each year; however, no one has ever died of a marijuana overdose.

Prevention Efforts

Government agencies, schools, and community organizations have mounted education and prevention campaigns to discourage young people from trying marijuana, but experts believe that the view of marijuana as harmless remains a major obstacle to antidrug efforts.

Overview

66With 100 million Americans having used pot at least once—including the president, his two immediate predecessors, the mayor of New York and countless other luminaries from all walks of life—and with an estimated 25 million regular users, marijuana consumption is a deeply ingrained pattern of American culture.99

—Norm Stamper, former police chief of Seattle, Washington, and a board member of Law Enforcement Against Prohibition.

66There's just not anything wrong with marijuana if you use it responsibly. . . . A lot of people will tell you, a lot of doctors will tell you—that it is a good medicine for stress.99

—Willie Nelson, country singer and cochair of the advisory board of NORML, an organization that supports marijuana legalization.

For many generations marijuana has been the most commonly used illicit drug in the United States, and it remains so today. In 2009 more than 28 million Americans (11.3 percent) aged 12 or older reported using marijuana within the past year, and 4.3 million met medical criteria for abuse or dependence.

For generations, debate has raged about whether marijuana should be made legal. While much of the debate is focused on the legalization of marijuana for medical purposes, some people believe that the drug should be allowed for recreational purposes as well.

Cannabis Sativa, the Source of Marijuana

Marijuana consists of the flowers and leafy parts of the hemp plant *Cannabis sativa*. For centuries this plant has been grown for its strong, fibrous stalk, used to make hemp rope, canvas, and cloth.

The term *cannabis*, however, generally refers to marijuana and other drugs made from the same plant. At least 66 different psychoactive ingredients—those that affect thinking, mood, or behavior—have been found in the cannabis plant. The main chemical that gives marijuana its narcotic effect is delta-9-tetrahydrocannabinol, or THC. THC is particularly strong in the resin, or sap, of the cannabis plant. This resin can

Marijuana consists of the flowers and leafy parts of the hemp plant Cannabis sativa. *Worldwide approximately 190 million people use cannabis, primarily for the narcotic effect of the chemical THC.*

be dried and compressed into a powdery paste called hashish, or hash, and smoked in a pipe. Hashish has more than five times the potency of a marijuana cigarette. Hash oil, a more concentrated form of cannabis resin, is even more potent.

How Marijuana Works

The most common way for marijuana to be consumed is by smoking the leaves. Dried leaves are rolled into a cigarette—or joint—or can be smoked through a pipe. Marijuana also can be smoked in a "blunt," a cigar wrapping from which the tobacco has been removed and which has been refilled with marijuana, sometimes in conjunction with another drug. Some users smoke marijuana leaves or hashish in a bong, a large pipe with a tube filled with water. The water cools off the smoke and makes it easier to inhale a harsh or strong drug.

When smoke from the marijuana is inhaled, the fumes carry the THC into the lungs. There THC binds to millions of alveoli, tiny sacs that absorb oxygen and pass it into the bloodstream. It takes only a few seconds for the THC to enter the bloodstream and reach the brain, giving users an immediate high.

Marijuana users also sometimes mix marijuana leaves into foods—most commonly baked goods. Usually, the leaves are shredded and baked into brownies or cookies. Marijuana can also be brewed as a tea. When the marijuana is swallowed, the THC enters the blood through the lining of the stomach. Although it takes longer for the THC to reach the bloodstream when it is ingested, once the THC does reach the bloodstream, the effect is the same as when it is smoked. The process of digestion causes the main active ingredient, delta-9-THC, to be transformed into delta-11-THC, which is more psychoactively powerful.

Users describe the impact of marijuana as a relaxing, peaceful feeling. Marijuana often has some unpleasant effects, however. The mellow high sometimes is followed by feelings of paranoia, anxiety, or panic.

A Brief History of Marijuana Use

People first used marijuana thousands of years ago. The cannabis plant is indigenous to Asia, and written records from China indicate that marijuana was used to treat pain, constipation, malaria, and a host of other illnesses more than 4,000 years ago. Ancient peoples in India, Greece, and other parts of the world used cannabis to treat a wide range of illnesses and as an appetite stimulant and sleep aid. There is also evidence that marijuana was used by some ancient cultures in religious ceremonies.

In the United States the use of cannabis dates back to colonial days. The settlers in Jamestown, Virginia, grew the plant as a source of hemp for rope, paper, clothing, and other uses. Hemp became so valuable that colonial governments passed laws requiring farmers to grow it. There is no evidence that early colonists used any other part of the plant, but by the early 1800s many Americans were using the leafy part of the cannabis plant for recreational and medicinal purposes. Physicians prescribed marijuana to treat a variety of ailments, from headaches to depression and insanity. From the middle to the late 1800s, when chemists learned how to mass-produce aspirin, marijuana was the most commonly prescribed pain medication in the United States.

> " **Ancient peoples in India, Greece, and other parts of the world used cannabis to treat a wide range of illnesses and as an appetite stimulant and sleep aid.** "

Early Marijuana Laws

By the twentieth century attitudes toward marijuana had changed. Newspapers published sensationalized stories about the use of marijuana and its damaging effects, and Americans worried about the drug's impact on young people. In 1913 California passed the first law banning the use of marijuana for recreational purposes; by 1930, 30 states had followed suit.

Sensational reports of the spread of marijuana and its links to crime played on the fears that marijuana was corrupting America's young people. In 1936 the government released *Reefer Madness*, a propaganda film that exaggerated the dangers of marijuana and warned parents and children against its use. A year later Congress passed the Marijuana Tax Act, which outlawed recreational use of marijuana and levied a hefty tax on hemp farmers. The taxes helped to put hemp farmers out of business or drive them underground.

Harry J. Anslinger, the director of the Federal Bureau of Narcotics in the 1930s, believed that marijuana was dangerous. Eight days after the Marijuana Tax Act went into effect, the Federal Bureau of Narcotics began arresting people for using marijuana. Within four months of the Marijuana Tax Act, federal agents had made almost 400 arrests.

Lawmakers and law enforcement officers seemed powerless to stop the spread of marijuana use. In 1956 Congress passed the Narcotics Control Act, which set a minimum sentence of two years in prison for marijuana possession, but the federal government appeared to be fighting a losing battle. During the 1960s, marijuana parties were a common part of college life. Thousands of hippies dropped out of school and joined the counterculture, a lifestyle that rebelled against the staid norms of their parents' generation. Experimenting with marijuana and other drugs was a key element of the counterculture. According to the New York Times, marijuana was used by 99 percent of the attendees at Woodstock, a three-day music festival held in upstate New York in 1969.

> From the middle to the late 1800s, when chemists learned how to mass-produce aspirin, marijuana was the most commonly prescribed pain medication in the United States.

In 1969 the Supreme Court ruled the Marijuana Tax Act of 1937 unconstitutional because it violated the Fifth Amendment protection against self-incrimination. Essentially, in order to comply with the tax, people had to admit that they were growing or selling marijuana, which was illegal.

Congress sought other means to restrict the use of marijuana and included it in the Controlled Substances Act of 1970. This act created five categories—or schedules—of drugs based on criteria such as a drug's potential for abuse and addiction and its accepted medical uses. Marijuana was classified as a Schedule I drug, the most dangerous and highly controlled category of drugs. Schedule I is reserved for drugs that have high potential for abuse and no currently accepted medical uses; other drugs in this category are highly addictive and dangerous drugs such as heroin and LSD.

The Controlled Substances Act establishes different penalties for violating drug laws in the different schedules of drugs, with harsher punishments for more dangerous drugs. Much of the debate regarding marijuana laws revolves around its placement in the most dangerous class of drugs. The Controlled Substances Act has been amended several times since 1970, but attempts to change marijuana's classification have failed.

Sources of Marijuana

One of the reasons that marijuana is so widely used is its relative ease of access. According to the US Drug Enforcement Administration (DEA), roughly half of all marijuana used in the United States is grown in America. The National Organization for the Reform of Marijuana Laws estimates that 9 million marijuana plants are grown in the United States each year, earning cultivators $15 billion. This makes marijuana a bigger cash crop than wheat, cotton, and tobacco combined. Statistics show that the primary states in which marijuana is cultivated are California, Hawaii, Kentucky, Oregon, Tennessee, Washington, and West Virginia. Marijuana is grown on rural farms and in suburban backyards. Extensive marijuana fields have also been found in national and state parks, forests, and other public lands. Marijuana also can be grown indoors, under bright lights that mimic the light and heat of the sun.

Marijuana is also smuggled into the United States from other countries. The largest exporters of marijuana appear to be Mexico, Jamaica, and Thailand, but marijuana plants are grown in a host of countries around the world. The most common method used by drug dealers is to smuggle the drugs across the border from Mexico or Canada. More security at the border has made importation more difficult, but experts estimate that tens of thousands of cars and trucks carry pot across the border every year. In addition to hiding marijuana in vehicles going through customs, smugglers have been known to build tunnels under the fences along the border. In 2006, for instance, authorities found a 0.5-mile-long (0.8km) tunnel that ran

> " According to the US Drug Enforcement Administration (DEA), roughly half of all marijuana used in the United States is grown in America. "

from Tijuana, Mexico, to Otay Mesa, California. Marijuana also enters the United States via off-road vehicles, boats, and planes.

The Supply Chain

The people growing marijuana are far from the only ones making money off the drug. Marijuana usually goes through many hands before reaching the end user. The marijuana business is highly organized. In Central and South America, marijuana is a key offering of huge drug cartels run by dangerous drug lords. In 1985 the DEA uncovered an operation that employed more than 12,000 people in cultivating, harvesting, packaging, and shipping marijuana to the United States. The sale of marijuana is often used to support the cultivation and sale of heroin, cocaine, and other street drugs.

> "The largest exporters of marijuana appear to be Mexico, Jamaica, and Thailand, but marijuana plants are grown in a host of countries around the world."

In the United States the local marijuana market is often controlled by gangs. Marijuana may go through a number of middlemen before reaching the street, where it is typically sold by the ounce. The price varies greatly from city to city, depending on how many middlemen are involved and the size of the market.

The sale of marijuana can be extremely profitable. Some people argue that gangs put the funds reaped from selling marijuana into buying or making more dangerous drugs. They believe that legalizing marijuana could help put the gangs out of business.

Is Marijuana a Dangerous Drug?

There is widespread debate over the dangers of marijuana. Antidrug advocates believe that even occasional marijuana use can have a devastating impact on the user's health. According to the National Institute on Drug Abuse, marijuana increases the risk of heart attack, stroke, and mental illness. Exposure to marijuana smoke may increase a person's risk of lung disease and respiratory illness.

Marijuana also may increase susceptibility to mental illness. Studies have shown that marijuana use contributes to antisocial thoughts and behaviors, as well as anxiety, depression, thoughts of suicide, schizophrenia, and other psychoses.

Marijuana may pose a particular danger to people who are driving or engaging in other high-risk behaviors, because the drug impedes judgment and hampers coordination. More drivers involved in automobile accidents have THC in their systems than any other drug except alcohol.

New Marijuana Strains

Marijuana growers have found ways to develop higher levels of THC in the plant's leaves and flowers; some health advocates believe the higher potency of marijuana today makes the drug more dangerous than ever. In 2007 the British magazine, the *Independent*, reported that it had reversed its position on decriminalization due to the dangers of a potent cannabis strain known as "skunk." "Record numbers of teenagers are requiring drug treatment as a result of smoking skunk, the highly potent cannabis strain that is 25 times stronger than resin sold a decade ago. . . . Doctors and drugs experts [warn] that skunk can be as damaging as cocaine and heroin, leading to mental health problems and psychosis for thousands of teenagers."[1]

> **Marijuana growers have found ways to develop higher levels of THC in the plant's leaves and flowers; some health advocates believe the higher potency of marijuana today makes the drug more dangerous than ever.**

Another concern relates to the rise of synthetic forms of marijuana that have recently arrived on America's streets. Commonly called K2, Spice, or Blaze, synthetic marijuana has become increasingly popular, particularly among teens. Until 2010 these substances were widely available in retail shops and over the Internet, often marketed as incense, but as reports began to circulate of adverse events resulting from their use, the US government took action to make their sale and use illegal.

Should Marijuana Be Legal for Medical Use?

In 2001 Canada became the first country in the world to legalize the use of marijuana for medical purposes. Canada's Marihuana Medical Access Regulations allow people suffering from grave and debilitating illnesses to use marijuana under a doctor's guidance. A 2001 study by the Medical Marijuana Information Resource Centre estimated that roughly 2 percent of Canadians were legally using marijuana with a doctor's permission.

In the United States 15 states, covering more than 27 percent of the US population, have enacted laws to allow the use of cannabis for medi-

Although experts disagree on the medical benefits of marijuana, when prescribed as a medical treatment it is most often used by patients with cancer, AIDS, and other debilitating diseases for relief of pain, nausea, and depression and anxiety.

cal purposes. These states have removed state-level criminal penalties for the cultivation, possession, and use of medical marijuana if use has been recommended by a medical doctor. Not all state laws are the same. In California, for instance, doctors have free rein in deciding the illnesses that can be treated with marijuana, but in Washington doctors can only prescribe marijuana to treat a list of very specific illnesses. Limitations on the amount of marijuana patients may possess vary from state to state as well.

Some local governments have also adopted medical marijuana laws that give authority to local agencies to regulate marijuana dispensaries.

> " **Opponents of legalization say that more people would use marijuana if it were a legal substance and that the increased use would result in more car accidents, health problems, and lost productivity, costing the country countless millions of dollars.** "

Most of these localities are in states that have passed laws allowing the use of marijuana for medical purposes, but localities in non-medical marijuana states have also acted. In November 2004 Ann Arbor, Michigan, became the first locality in that state to pass a medical marijuana law; since then four other Michigan cities—including Detroit—have followed suit. Experts suggest that local laws demonstrate a change in the priorities of law enforcement. "Although largely symbolic, such local laws can influence the priorities of local law enforcement officers and prosecutors,"[2] concludes a Congressional Research Service report.

Under federal law, the use of marijuana—even when prescribed by a doctor—is illegal. For the most part the federal government has turned a blind eye to use that is in accordance with state laws. In a memo dated October 19, 2009, the US Department of Justice advised federal prosecutors not to target patients whose actions are in compliance with state laws legalizing the use of marijuana for medical use.

Some Americans go beyond advocating marijuana for medical use to argue that it should be legal for Americans to use marijuana for recreational purposes as well. Legalization advocates say that it is impossible to eliminate marijuana use and compare efforts to do so to the prohibition of alcohol in the 1920s. They argue that marijuana is less dangerous than alcohol, cigarettes, and other legal substances.

Opponents of legalization say that more people would use marijuana if it were a legal substance and that the increased use would result in more car accidents, health problems, and lost productivity, costing the country countless millions of dollars. Proponents of legalization argue that it would enable the government to regulate the sale of marijuana, whereas opponents believe that legalization would add to the government's regulatory burden. Some opponents of legalization also argue that making the drug legal would simply add to the number of customers for illegal dealers and drug cartels.

How Effective Are Efforts to Prevent Marijuana Use?

The US government spends billions of dollars trying to prevent marijuana use. Millions more are spent trying to rehabilitate marijuana addicts. More people are in treatment for marijuana addiction than for addiction to any other type of illegal drug.

Many people believe that reducing the rate of marijuana use will require addressing supply. In a recent survey of teens, more than half of respondents between the ages of 12 and 17 said that marijuana was easy to obtain. Prevention among young people also will require addressing demand. Antidrug advocates say that educating young people about the dangers of marijuana is a key element of any strategy focused on curbing future use.

Marijuana continues to provoke controversy. The federal government has fought to eradicate the use of marijuana for many years—an effort that an increasing number of Americans believe to be futile. Increasing numbers of people argue that a more realistic approach to reducing marijuana use would rely on education and treatment. Still others advocate making marijuana legal altogether, putting the drug into the hands of responsible parties and regulators. At the center of the debate is the impact that marijuana has on a person's health, whether the potential benefits of its use outweigh its health risks, and whether targeting the illegal sale and use of the drug is a good use of government funds.

Is Marijuana a Dangerous Drug?

> 66 The science, though still evolving, is clear: marijuana use is harmful. It is associated with dependence, respiratory and mental illness, poor motor performance, and cognitive impairment, among other negative effects. 99

—R. Gil Kerlikowske, director of the Office of National Drug Control Policy.

> 66 Marijuana is a remarkably safe drug. . . . Unlike other psychoactive drugs, including alcohol, aspirin, opiates, nicotine, and caffeine, cannabis is not known to cause fatal overdoses. 99

—Gregory T. Carter and Dale Gieringer, authors of *Marijuana Medical Handbook: Practical Guide to Therapeutic Uses of Marijuana.*

Much of the controversy around marijuana stems from disagreement about its health risks. Anecdotal evidence and research studies have shown that marijuana use can impair memory and cognition, but scientists disagree on whether these functions are affected over the long term. Some studies suggest there may be a link between marijuana use—particularly at a young age—and various forms of mental illness. Researchers also disagree about whether smoking marijuana contributes to lung disease, cancer, and other debilitating diseases.

THC and the Brain

THC—the main psychoactive ingredient in marijuana—affects behavior by acting on the chemicals in the brain that dictate a person's thoughts and actions. In the brain 100 billion neurons transmit messages in the form of neurotransmitters, chemicals that bridge the synapses—the small narrow gaps that separate the neurons. These chemical messengers travel across the neurons at an amazing rate of speed—less than 1/5,000 of a second—allowing people to react instantaneously and unconsciously to pain or other stimuli. Neurotransmitters travel from neuron to neuron in an orderly fashion. They are specifically shaped so that after they pass from a neuron into the synapse, they can be received onto certain sites, called receptors, on another neuron.

THC acts by attaching to cannabinoid receptors that are found in high concentrations in the hippocampus, cerebellum, and basal ganglia—the parts of the brain that influence pleasure, memory, concentration, sensory and time perception, and coordination. When THC binds with the cannabinoid receptors in the hippocampus, it interferes with the natural function of neurotransmitters to store and retrieve messages, impairing short-term memory and learning. Users also often experience increased heart rate and lower blood pressure. Other common effects include hunger and food cravings that have come to be known as "the munchies." THC similarly interferes with neurotransmitters in the cerebellum, which controls body movements, and the basal ganglia, which controls unconscious muscle movements. This is why marijuana users often lack good physical coordination.

> While there is no clear link between marijuana use and violence or dangerous behavior, there is evidence that THC reduces inhibitions, which can lead to violent outbursts among people who are already predisposed to such behavior.

Marijuana users come down from their high after a couple of hours, but THC can remain in the system for as long as 10 days before being broken down. The impact of marijuana use may extend far beyond these 10 days, however. Some experts believe that THC can cause structural changes to the hippocampus and damage nerve cells. Studies have shown that long-term, frequent marijuana users have lower IQs than nonsmoking populations.

Behavior

Marijuana has an immediate impact on one's mood and emotions. Marijuana users sometimes are overcome by laughter or tears—perhaps switching from one extreme to another with little reason. The sudden change in emotions has to do with the way that THC affects the limbic system, the area of the brain that controls emotions. Studies show that THC inhibits the brain's release of serotonin, a neurotransmitter that helps regulate mood, emotions, sleep, and appetite. THC can interfere with the body's natural impulses in these areas, contributing to mood swings, emotional instability, and sleepiness or insomnia.

While there is no clear link between marijuana use and violence or dangerous behavior, there is evidence that THC reduces inhibitions, which can lead to violent outbursts among people who are already predisposed to such behavior. Experts caution that these risks may be higher with recently developed strains, such as skunk, than with more typical strains of the drug. In addition, marijuana is often used in combination with alcohol or other drugs, increasing the risk of antisocial behavior.

There is also evidence that marijuana may reduce inhibitions that influence sexual behavior, especially in young people. Studies suggest that users are more likely to engage in unsafe sex, putting them at greater risk of sexually transmitted diseases. Some experts cite evidence that there is a correlation between drug use, including marijuana, and the spread of HIV.

> Chronic marijuana use is associated with apathy, indecisiveness, and loss of ambition or interest in pursuing personal goals, all of which are obstacles to educational achievement and success on the job.

Chronic marijuana use also is associated with apathy, indecisiveness, and loss of ambition or interest in pursuing personal goals, all of which are obstacles to educational achievement and success on the job. According to the National Institute on Drug Abuse, teens who smoke marijuana have lower grades, have higher rates of absenteeism from school, and are less likely to graduate from high school than their peers who do not use drugs. Marijuana users also report less satisfaction with school and extra-curricular activities. Similarly, adult marijuana users are more likely to be unemployed than those who do not use the drug.

Critics question the assumption that marijuana use contributes to poor school performance. Some suggest that the reverse is true: Teens who have negative attitudes toward school and a lack of motivation to succeed may be more likely to use marijuana.

Impact on Mental Health

Marijuana users often suffer from panic attacks and paranoia, and longer-term use may have a more profound impact on one's mental health. For instance, studies show that adults who use marijuana are more likely to suffer from anxiety and depression than adults who do not use marijuana. While some experts conclude that marijuana use increases the risk of depression or anxiety, others say that people suffering from these disorders may turn to marijuana to help alleviate their symptoms.

Research suggests there may also be a link between marijuana use and schizophrenia and other psychotic disorders. Researchers caution that while marijuana use may not *cause* mental illness, it may contribute to the severity and earlier onset of psychoses in people who have a genetic predisposition. Some studies have shown the age at which people first use marijuana to be a factor: The younger people are when they start using the drug, the more vulnerable they may be to mental illness.

> Like people with other addictions, chronic marijuana users may become obsessed with finding and obtaining the drug at any cost.

Some studies suggest that chronic marijuana use among young people is higher among victims of abuse or trauma or those living under a great deal of stress. Scientists believe these studies support the theory that people sometimes use the drug to help deal with overwhelmingly unpleasant feelings. In fact, some experts believe that, used in moderation, marijuana may help people overcome social anxiety and depression to better function in society.

Physical Effects

Physicians warn that extended marijuana use can cause a variety of health-related problems. Marijuana users appear to be more susceptible than nonusers to colds, the flu, and other illnesses, and their recovery time from illness is often slower than average. Marijuana smoke irritates the lungs, increasing the risk of chronic asthma and bronchitis, an irritation and inflammation of the airways in the lungs, as well as emphysema, a disease in which the tiny air sacs in the lungs are damaged, making it difficult for oxygen to pass from the lungs into the bloodstream. Some physicians caution that people who smoke marijuana may be even more susceptible to these illnesses than those who smoke cigarettes because marijuana smokers inhale the smoke more deeply into their lungs and hold the smoke longer than cigarette smokers do.

Some doctors warn that heavy use of marijuana interferes with hormones. In animal studies, marijuana has been linked to lower testosterone levels and sperm count in men. Critics of these studies say that they exaggerate the impact of marijuana: The amount of drugs used in testing is far higher than would be used by humans. "It is possible that adolescents are peculiarly vulnerable to hormonal disruptions from pot," concedes Dale Gieringer, the coordinator of NORML in California. "However, not a single case of impaired fertility has ever been observed in humans of either sex."[3] Warnings that marijuana use during pregnancy may cause miscarriage or birth defects have also been criticized. Advocates of legalization counter that, conversely, marijuana may help ease the anxiety and nausea that are often associated with pregnancy.

> " Experts point out that while many drug users begin with marijuana, this does not mean that there is a clear cause-and-effect relationship between marijuana and other drug use. In fact, a very small percentage of people who try marijuana go on to abuse other drugs. "

Marijuana and Cancer

Some health advocates warn that smoking marijuana has the same risks as smoking cigarettes. According to the American Cancer Society, "Smoking damages nearly every organ in the human body, is linked to at least 15 different cancers, and accounts for some 30 percent of all cancer deaths."[4] Because marijuana contains toxins and carcinogens, marijuana smokers increase their risk of cancer of the head, neck, lungs, and respiratory tract.

Evidence that smoking marijuana contributes to cancer is inconclusive, however. In 2006 the largest study of its kind concluded that smoking marijuana, even regularly and heavily, does not lead to lung cancer. Lead researcher Donald Tashkin noted that the findings were not what researchers anticipated. "We hypothesized that there would be a positive association between marijuana and lung cancer," Tashkin noted. "What we found instead was no association at all, and even a suggestion of some protective effect."[5] In a 2009 report published by the American Association for Cancer Research, the authors write of their findings:

> We found that moderate marijuana use was significantly associated with reduced risk of HNSCC [head and neck squamous cell carcinoma]. This association was consistent across different measures of marijuana use (marijuana use status, duration, and frequency of use). . . . Further, we observed that marijuana use modified the interaction between alcohol and cigarette smoking, resulting in a decreased HNSCC risk among moderate smokers and light drinkers, and attenuated risk among the heaviest smokers and drinkers.[6]

Marijuana Addiction

Some people argue that marijuana is less physically addictive than other street drugs, but many people become dependent on the emotional high the drug provides. "Like any other powerful, mood altering substance, people who are prone to chemical dependency can become addicted to marijuana," cautions the Alcohol Drug Abuse Resource Center, which provides online information about alcohol and drug addiction. "The thing about marijuana is it is very subtle. You can use it daily, for extended periods of time and think nothing of it. Yet the person has become completely dependent and doesn't even realize it."[7]

Like people with other addictions, chronic marijuana users may become obsessed with finding and obtaining the drug at any cost. They may be unable to cease drug use even when they recognize that the drug is interfering with work or other aspects of their lives. As the body becomes accustomed to marijuana, tolerance increases and users require more of the drug to obtain the same high. As a result, users may start consuming ever-increasing quantities of marijuana at increasing frequency.

Users who quit using marijuana may experience withdrawal symptoms ranging from irritability to headaches, insomnia, decreased appetite, and anxiety. The intensity of these symptoms can last anywhere from a few days to a week, depending on the frequency and duration of use. These withdrawal symptoms typically peak at two or three days after stopping marijuana use and subside within a week or two, but experts caution that longtime users may crave the drug long beyond this period of time.

Marijuana as a Gateway Drug

A major concern of opponents of marijuana is that using marijuana increases the risk of moving to more dangerous street drugs such as cocaine and heroin. A number of studies have confirmed that young substance abusers usually follow a sequence of drug use: from alcohol and tobacco to marijuana to other drugs such as cocaine and heroin. Research undertaken by the Substance Abuse and Mental Health Services Administration, a federal government agency that studies drug abuse, also shows that the younger a child is when first using marijuana, the more likely he or she is to use other street drugs and to become dependent on these drugs.

Experts point out that while many drug users begin with marijuana, this does not mean that there is a clear cause-and-effect relationship between marijuana and other drug use. In fact, a very small percentage of people who try marijuana go on to abuse other drugs. A 2010 study of Californians seeking marijuana for medical purposes found that many of these people had used marijuana in the past "at modest levels and in consistent patterns which anecdotally often assisted their educational achievement, employment performance, and establishment of a more stable lifestyle."[8] The authors conclude, "These data suggest that rather than acting as a gateway to other drugs, . . . cannabis has been exerting a beneficial influence on most."[9] Debunking the theory that marijuana contributes to drug problems and abuse has been an integral strategy for people seeking legalization of the drug for medical and recreational purposes.

Primary Source Quotes*

Is Marijuana a Dangerous Drug?

> **66** Rising levels in cannabis potency in many parts of the world (notably in industrialized countries) have also contributed to the increased risk of cannabis use.**99**

—United Nations Office on Drugs and Crime, *World Drug Report 2010*. www.unodc.org.

The United Nations Office on Drugs and Crime engages in multilateral partnerships to combat international problems related to drugs and crime.

> **66** The growing fears over the past five years concerning the 'new potency' of cannabis have . . . been based largely on anecdote and conjecture.**99**

—Charlie Lloyd and Neil McKeganey, *Drugs Research: An Overview of Evidence and Questions for Policy*. London: Joseph Rowntree Foundation, June 2010. www.jrf.org.uk.

Lloyd is a researcher on drug and alcohol issues and a senior lecturer at the University of York; McKeganey is with the Centre for Drug Misuse Research at the University of Glasgow.

Bracketed quotes indicate conflicting positions.

* Editor's Note: While the definition of a primary source can be narrowly or broadly defined, for the purposes of Compact Research, a primary source consists of: 1) results of original research presented by an organization or researcher; 2) eyewitness accounts of events, personal experience, or work experience; 3) first-person editorials offering pundits' opinions; 4) government officials presenting political plans and/or policies; 5) representatives of organizations presenting testimony or policy.

❝Since 1982, I have treated literally several thousand individuals suffering from all varieties of addiction, including marijuana dependency and abuse. From this clinical experience, I have taken away a strong conviction that marijuana is dangerous.❞

—Charles V. Giannasio, "Marijuana & Money: Marijuana Is Addictive, Destructive and Dangerous," CNBC, April 20, 2010. www.cnbc.com.

Giannasio is a physician specializing in addiction psychiatry.

❝Marijuana is far less dangerous than alcohol or tobacco. Around 50,000 people die each year from alcohol poisoning. Similarly, more than 400,000 deaths each year are attributed to tobacco smoking. By comparison, marijuana is nontoxic and cannot cause death by overdose.❞

—NORML, "About Marijuana," November 7, 2010. http://norml.org.

The National Organization for the Reform of Marijuana Laws is a leading lobbying group for legalization of marijuana.

❝Someone who smokes marijuana every day may be functioning at a suboptimal intellectual level all of the time.❞

—National Institute on Drug Abuse, "NIDA InfoFacts: Marijuana," November 2011. www.nida.nih.gov.

The National Institute on Drug Abuse supports and conducts extensive scientific research on drug abuse and addiction.

❝Marijuana has indisputably been shown to increase the risk for schizophrenia. Kids, when they smoke marijuana during adolescence, are doubling, tripling, or quadrupling their chances of developing schizophrenia.❞

—Jeffrey Lieberman, "Is Schizophrenia Preventable?" EmpowHER, August 17, 2009. www.empowher.com.

Lieberman is chair of the Department of Psychiatry at the Columbia University College of Physicians and Surgeons, director of the New York State Psychiatric Institute, and director of the Lieber Center for Schizophrenia Research.

66 [Our] study does not support the specific causal link between cannabis use and the incidence of psychotic disorders. . . . This concurs with other reports indicating that increases in population cannabis use have not been followed by increases in psychotic incidence. 99

—Martin Frisher et al., "Assessing the Impact of Cannabis Use on Trends in Diagnosed Schizophrenia in the United Kingdom from 1996 to 2005," United Kingdom Schizophrenia Research, 2009. www.ukcia.org.

Frisher and his study colleagues are professors and researchers at Keele University in Staffordshire, England.

66 Cannabis use is more strongly associated with other illicit drug use than alcohol or tobacco use, and the earliest and most frequent cannabis users are the most likely to use other illicit drugs. 99

—Robin Room et al., *Cannabis Policy: Moving Beyond Stalemate.* Oxford: Oxford University Press, 2010.

The authors came together on behalf of the Beckley Foundation, which works to develop a base of scientific evidence on which drug policy can be based.

66 The public health burden of cannabis use is probably modest compared with that of alcohol, tobacco, and other illicit drugs. 99

—Wayne Hall and Louisa Degenhardt, "Adverse Health Effects of Non-Medical Cannabis Use," *Lancet*, October 17, 2009. http://science.iowamedicalmarijuana.org.

Hall is a professor of public health policy at the University of Queensland, Australia; Degenhardt is a researcher and professor with the National Drug and Alcohol Research Centre at the University of New South Wales in Sydney.

66 Although marijuana is sometimes characterized as a 'harmless herb,' the cultivation, trafficking, and use of the drug have a negative impact on many aspects of our lives, from public health to national security, transportation, the environment, and educational attainment. 99

—Office of National Drug Control Policy, "Marijuana: Know the Facts," October 2010. www.whitehousedrugpolicy.gov.

The Office of National Drug Control Policy is the White House office responsible for drug policy.

"Overall, Americans feel that persons who are addicted to ... cocaine and heroin are much more of a danger to society than those addicted to marijuana."

— Substance Abuse and Mental Health Services Administration, "Americans Believe in Prevention and Recovery from Addictions," 2008 survey data. http://www.samhsa.gov.

SAMHSA is an agency of the US Department of Health and Human Services that supports programs to improve the lives of people with or at risk for mental illness and substance use disorders.

Is Marijuana a Dangerous Drug?

- According to the National Survey on Drug Use and Health, more than **4.3 million** Americans meet the medical criteria for marijuana abuse or dependence.

- A 2010 study conducted by the Queensland Brain Institute in Australia found that young people who smoke cannabis or marijuana for six years or more are twice as likely to have **psychotic episodes, hallucinations, or delusions** than people who have never used the drug.

- In a study of participants in the Baltimore, Maryland, area and published in the *American Journal of Psychiatry*, four times as many marijuana users than nonusers suffer from **major depression**.

- In a study of 70 participants aged 17 to 23, the **average IQ** of participants who smoked 5 or more joints per week decreased an average of 4 points.

- According to government data, the average potency of marijuana has more than doubled since 1998. The University of Mississippi's Potency Monitoring Project shows that the percentage of THC in street marijuana in 2010 was **10.1 percent**, compared to **4 percent** the early 1980s.

- The Drug Abuse Warning Network (DAWN), a system for monitoring the health impact of drugs, shows that each year nearly 374,000 Americans who visit an **emergency room** report marijuana as the primary problem.

Evidence of Addiction

Some experts cite the growing number of people seeking treatment for marijuana abuse as evidence of the drug's addictive properties. According to study findings published in 2010, more teens seek treatment for marijuana use than for any other substance, including alcohol. As shown on this chart, of the 372 teens admitted to federally funded treatment facilities on an average day, 263 sought treatment for marijuana use — far more than for all other substances combined.

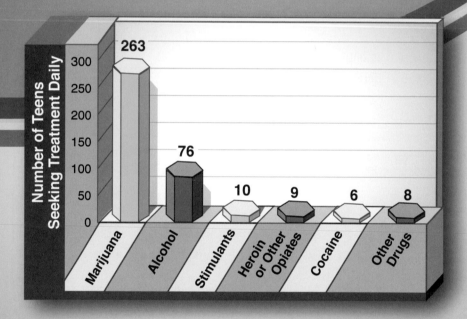

Source: SAMHSA Office of Applied Studies, "A Day in the Life of American Adolescents: Substance Use Facts Update," April 29, 2010. www.oas.samhsa.gov.

- There are **no documented deaths** resulting from marijuana. Estimates on how much marijuana would amount to a **fatal dose** vary widely: some studies suggest that a 150-pound (68kg) person would have to eat **46 pounds** (21kg) of marijuana, while others say that at least **1,500 pounds** (680kg) would be needed.

Marijuana Potency on the Rise

In recent decades, marijuana growers have been genetically altering their plants to increase the percentage of THC, the main active chemical in marijuana. THC acts upon the brain in a variety of ways, negatively impacting coordination, perception, thinking, concentration, and memory. Some health experts warn that the increasing amount of THC in marijuana makes the drug more dangerous than ever. As shown by this graph, the average potency of the marijuana seized by federal officials has doubled since 1998.

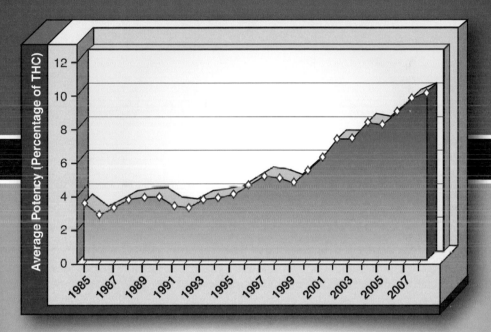

Source: National Center for Natural Products Research, Research Institute of Pharmaceutical Sciences, University of Mississippi, *Quarterly Report, Potency Monitoring Project*, Report 107, January 12, 2010.

- Most studies comparing children of marijuana users with those of nonusers show **no difference** in birth weight, cognitive ability, cancer rates, or other factors.

- A study conducted by the University of Auckland in New Zealand found that habitual marijuana users were **9.5 times more likely** to be involved in **car accidents** than people who did not use marijuana.

Marijuana as a Gateway Drug?

Statistics from the National Survey on Drug Use and Health show that a significant number of first-time drug users begin with marijuana. Whether marijuana can be considered a gateway drug, meaning that people who smoke marijuana go on to other, more dangerous drugs, is up for debate. Some experts contend that marijuana plays this role while others say that only a small percentage of people who try marijuana go on to use other drugs.

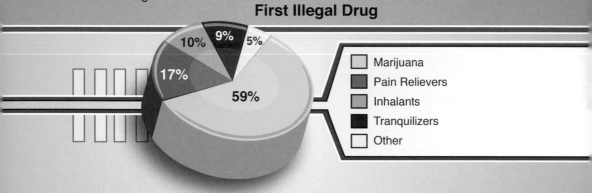

First Illegal Drug

- 10%
- 9%
- 5%
- 17%
- 59%

Legend:
- Marijuana
- Pain Relievers
- Inhalants
- Tranquilizers
- Other

Source: Substance Abuse and Mental Health Services Administration, *Results from the 2009 National Survey on Drug Use and Health: Volume I: Summary of National Findings*, September 2010. www.oas.samhsa.gov.

- A 2008 study undertaken by the Dutch Institute for Road Safety Research found that marijuana alone **does not increase** the risk of **accidents**.

- A report undertaken by the Substance Abuse and Mental Health Services Administration found that **62 percent** of adults who used marijuana before age 15 went on to use cocaine at some point in their lives; **9 percent** went on to use heroin at least once; and **54 percent** engaged in nonmedical use of prescription drugs.

- A majority—**59.1 percent**—of the 3.1 million persons aged 12 or older using illicit drugs for the first time in the previous 12 months in the 2009 National Survey on Drug Use and Health reported that their first drug was marijuana.

Should Marijuana Be Legal for Medical Use?

66 Marijuana is effective at relieving nausea and vomiting, spasticity, appetite loss, certain types of pain, and other debilitating symptoms. And it is extraordinarily safe—safer than most medicines prescribed every day. If marijuana were a new discovery rather than a well-known substance carrying cultural and political baggage, it would be hailed as a wonder drug. 99

—Lester Grinspoon, professor emeritus of psychiatry at Harvard Medical School and author of several books on medical marijuana.

66 While smoking marijuana may allow patients to temporarily feel better, the medical community makes an important distinction between inebriation and the controlled delivery of pure pharmaceutical medication. The raw (leaf) form of marijuana contains a complex mixture of compounds in uncertain concentrations, the majority of which have unknown pharmacological effects. 99

—Office of National Drug Control Policy, the White House office responsible for drug policy.

In the United States there is widespread public support for the use of marijuana in medical treatment. In a 2010 public opinion poll conducted by ABC News and the *Washington Post*, more than four-fifths of respondents (81 percent) said they supported making marijuana legally available for medical use. Former US surgeon general Joycelyn Elders is among the supporters of legalizing marijuana for medical purposes: "The evidence is overwhelming that marijuana can relieve certain types of pain, nausea, vomiting and other symptoms caused by illnesses such as multiple sclerosis, cancer and AIDS—or by the harsh drugs sometimes used to treat them. And it can do so with remarkable safety."[10]

Limitations on Research

The debate over medical marijuana is stymied by a lack of clinical research. Because marijuana is classified as a Schedule I drug, researchers are largely unable to conduct controlled studies on humans. As a result, people on both sides of the issue continue to debate the findings of one of the few comprehensive studies, which was conducted in 1999 by the Institute of Medicine. The study concluded that some of the chemicals in marijuana could have significant value for terminally ill patients. The report's authors write, "For patients such as those with AIDS or who are undergoing chemotherapy, and who suffer simultaneously from severe pain, nausea, and appetite loss, cannabinoid drugs might offer broad-spectrum relief not found in any other single medication."[11]

> Scientific studies have suggested that marijuana controls nausea in cancer patients undergoing chemotherapy, reduces nausea and vomiting caused by AIDS or AIDS medication, and helps stimulate appetite in cancer and AIDS patients.

The Institute of Medicine stopped short of recommending smoking marijuana as a remedy, however, and a subsequent report from the institute declared that marijuana was not modern medicine because the words *medicine* and *marijuana* had opposite meanings. "Burning leaves is not a modern drug delivery system, period," adds Robert L. DuPont, former president of the National Institute for Drug Abuse. "'Medical marijuana' is an oxymoron."[12]

Recent research has focused on some of the potential advantages of marijuana. Scientific studies published in peer-reviewed medical journals have suggested that marijuana controls nausea in cancer patients undergoing chemotherapy, reduces nausea and vomiting caused by AIDS or AIDS medication, and helps stimulate appetite in cancer and AIDS patients. Marijuana also has been shown to reduce the pressure on the eye among glaucoma patients and to relieve muscle stiffness and spasms caused by

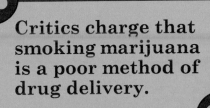

> Critics charge that smoking marijuana is a poor method of drug delivery.

multiple sclerosis. Marijuana relieves chronic pain associated with a wide range of debilitating illnesses. Some research has shown that marijuana may reduce dementia in people with Alzheimer's disease. In 2009 the American Medical Association, which had publicly opposed medical marijuana, modified its position to advocate "that marijuana's status as a federal Schedule I controlled substance be reviewed with the goal of facilitating the conduct of clinical research and development of cannabinoid-based medicines."[13]

Some advocates of medical marijuana also point out that risks are irrelevant to patients facing terminal illness. Medical marijuana, they say, offers a way for doctors to reduce suffering at the end of these patients' lives. For some patients marijuana may have pain-relieving benefit equal to that of morphine and other drugs, with far fewer adverse side effects.

Drug Delivery Problems

One of the problems with using marijuana as medicine is that users often smoke it. Critics charge that smoking marijuana is a poor method of drug delivery. One problem is that precise dosage is impossible. When a person smokes, the amount of drug they consume depends on how much and how deeply they inhale. Moreover, the harmful chemicals and carcinogens that are by-products of smoking may create entirely new health problems, such as lung cancer or respiratory illness. DuPont says, "There is no acceptable role in modern medicine for using burning leaves as a drug delivery system because smoke is inherently unhealthy."[14]

Defenders of medical marijuana say that it does not have to be smoked. Mixing or baking crushed marijuana leaves in food can help medical marijuana users avoid the dangers associated with inhaling smoke. Many patients say that tea made with marijuana leaves is particularly soothing for nausea. The growing number of people with prescriptions for medical marijuana has led to a new industry of edible marijuana products. Small businesses in states with medical marijuana laws have led the way in incorporating marijuana into candy, brownies, ice cream, soda, and even pizza sold to dispensaries that then sell the goods to patients with a prescription. Denver, Colorado, boasts the nation's first medical marijuana take-out restaurant. Since marijuana is still illegal under federal law, these products cannot cross state lines. For those who do not have access to these goods, there are an increasing number of recipes on the Internet and in bookstores. *Aunt Sandy's Medical Marijuana Cookbook*, for instance, includes information about the maladies that marijuana may relieve, tips about cooking safely with marijuana, and recipes for everything from soups and sauces, to chicken and pork dishes, to salty snacks and sweets.

> " Antidrug advocates believe that synthetic versions offer a safer alternative to marijuana. "

The Drug Free America Foundation cautions that eating or drinking marijuana is no safer than smoking it: "Eating [marijuana] delivers the same damaging compounds as well as the insecticides and fungi found in unmonitored crops."[15]

Synthetic THC

Pharmaceutical companies have begun to patent synthetic versions of desirable active agents that are found naturally in marijuana. In 2010 Great Britain became the first country to approve a synthetic form of marijuana called Sativex. In the United States the US Food and Drug Administration has approved Marinol (dronabinol), a synthetic pharmaceutical drug that contains delta-9 THC, as an appetite stimulant and for nausea in cancer, AIDS, and other ill patients. Marinol is currently available in the form of a pill; researchers are exploring the possibility of delivering the drug through an inhaler or a patch.

Antidrug advocates believe that these synthetic versions offer a safer alternative to marijuana. The DEA's website differentiates Marinol from marijuana: "Unlike smoked marijuana—which contains more than 400 different chemicals, including most of the hazardous chemicals found in tobacco smoke—Marinol has been studied and approved by the medical community and the Food and Drug Administration (FDA), the nation's watchdog over unsafe and harmful food and drug products."[16]

Marinol and other synthetic forms of the drug have their critics, however. Defenders of medical marijuana caution that synthetic marijuana has its own drawbacks. Some users complain that Marinol and Sativex are not as effective as marijuana, particularly in reducing nausea associated with chemotherapy or AIDS. Other users report that the psychoactive effects of synthetic drugs are far greater than those of natural cannabis. Adverse effects include drowsiness, dizziness, confusion, anxiety, changes in mood, muddled thinking, perceptual difficulties, coordination impairment, irritability, and depression.

> " **Whereas marijuana is relatively easy and inexpensive to cultivate naturally, manufacturing synthetic THC is extremely costly. Much of the cost is passed on to patients.** "

Another criticism of synthetic forms of THC is the cost. Whereas marijuana is relatively easy and inexpensive to cultivate naturally, manufacturing synthetic THC is extremely costly. Much of the cost is passed on to patients. For patients who are prescribed Marinol as part of a daily regimen of drugs, the cost can be prohibitive. "Marinol would do nothing for me," says a 66-year-old polio victim who was confined to a wheelchair before being prescribed medical marijuana. "It costs $970 a month while my marijuana costs $900 a year and it is totally like THC."[17]

People defending legalization of medical marijuana add that money is a key reason why there is so much opposition. They are quick to point out that pharmaceutical companies stand to lose millions of dollars if marijuana becomes standard treatment for illnesses currently treated with prescription drugs.

Medical Marijuana Dispensaries

Some Americans are concerned about having a medical marijuana dispensary in their neighborhood. They worry that such dispensaries will attract the "wrong" people and lead to an increase in crime. Some communities in states with medical marijuana laws have passed laws banning marijuana dispensaries.

The medical marijuana lobby says such fears are unfounded, and there is little evidence of increased crime in communities in which there are medical marijuana dispensaries. "We've had zero incidents in Sebastopol," says Craig Litwin, the California city's former mayor, of its dispensaries. "If there is a problem, we shut them down. I believe regulation is far superior to turning a blind eye."[18]

Some state and local governments view a tax on the sale of medical marijuana as a much-needed source of revenue. In a 2010 study Colorado Springs reported earnings of more than $50,000 a month in sales tax revenues; Boulder, home of the University of Colorado, estimated 2010 earnings of more than $400,000. In addition to the amounts received by local communities, the state of Colorado received $2.2 million in tax revenue in 2010 and an additional $8.5 million in fees.

Who Uses Medical Marijuana?

Determining exactly how many patients use medical marijuana with state approval is difficult, but data suggest the number is rising rapidly. Some experts believe that some people with prescriptions are using the drug for recreational purposes. The Drug Free America Foundation cautions, "In states with marijuana dispensaries, the vast majority of 'patients' are young men between the ages of 18 and 25, not the cancer or AIDS victims used in voter ads to exploit our compassionate nature."[19]

Still, ill patients defend legalization, sharing stories of the profound impact marijuana has had on their lives. Angel Raich, who sued the federal government in 2005 to allow her to continue using marijuana as part of her treatment for an inoperable brain tumor, tells of marijuana's unique role in the treatment of her disease:

> I suffer greatly from severe chronic pain every single day. The prolonged pain and suffering from my medical conditions significantly interferes with my quality of life. My

treatment is complicated by the fact that I am violently allergic and have severe multiple chemical sensitivities to almost all pharmaceutical medicines. This interferes with the treatment of all of my medical conditions, and it means my suffering cannot be controlled by synthetic medications. . . . Without cannabis my life would be a death sentence.[20]

Does Allowing Medical Marijuana Increase Use?

Antidrug advocates argue that allowing an illicit substance for any purpose gives young people the wrong message. "If young people don't really perceive that [marijuana] is dangerous or of any concern, it usually means there'll be an uptick in the number of kids who are using. And sure enough, in 2009, that's exactly what we did see,"[21] says R. Gil Kerlikowske, the head of the Office of National Drug Control Policy.

Still, evidence shows that the rate of marijuana use among teens in states where medical marijuana is allowed is no higher than where it remains illegal. NORML Advisory Board member Mitch Earleywine, who coauthored a comprehensive review of data on marijuana use, writes, "More than a decade after the passage of the nation's first state medical marijuana law, . . . a considerable body of data shows that no state with a medical marijuana law has experienced an increase in youth marijuana use since its law's enactment. All states have reported overall decreases—exceeding 50 percent in some age groups, strongly suggesting that the enactment of state medical marijuana laws does not increase marijuana use."[22]

In a study undertaken by the Texas A&M Health Science Center, researchers also concluded that medical marijuana laws "do not appear to increase use of the drug."[23] In fact, researchers speculate that linking marijuana to sickness might deter use by deglamorizing the drug.

The Future of the Debate

Throughout the United States—and beyond—the debate over medical marijuana continues. Medical researchers, physicians, and professional associations have spoken out on both sides of the issue. The American Academy of Family Physicians, the American Nurses Association, the American Public Health Organization, and the *New England Journal of*

Medicine are among those advocating for laws allowing the use of marijuana for medical purposes. On the other side of the debate, the National Cancer Institute, the American Cancer Society, and the National Multiple Sclerosis Society have stated publicly that they do not believe that the scientific evidence on the therapeutic use of marijuana meets the current standard of prescribed medicine.

Given the entrenched positions on both sides, the issue is likely to be hammered out in states and communities throughout the country. The issue is likely to resurface in the halls of Congress as well, where hearings allow people on both sides of the issue to tell stories about how medical marijuana has changed their lives.

Should Marijuana Be Legal for Medical Use?

> 66 Thousands of patients and their doctors have found marijuana to be beneficial in treating the symptoms of AIDS, cancer, multiple sclerosis, glaucoma, and other serious conditions. For many people, marijuana is the only medicine with a suitable degree of safety and efficacy. 99

—Marijuana Policy Project, *State by State Medical Marijuana Laws*, 2010. www.mpp.org.

The Marijuana Policy Project is the leading national sponsor of ballot initiatives and lobbying campaigns to reform marijuana laws.

> 66 People who need alternative therapies for pain relief and other symptoms associated with end-stage illness have plenty of options that don't require them to smoke [marijuana]. 99

—Dora Dixie, "Letter: Smoking Marijuana Is Not Medicine," *State Journal-Register* (Springfield, Ill.), January 20, 2011. www.sj-r.com.

Dixie is a family physician who specializes in addiction treatment and who served as president of the Illinois Society of Addiction Medicine in Chicago.

Bracketed quotes indicate conflicting positions.

* Editor's Note: While the definition of a primary source can be narrowly or broadly defined, for the purposes of Compact Research, a primary source consists of: 1) results of original research presented by an organization or researcher; 2) eyewitness accounts of events, personal experience, or work experience; 3) first-person editorials offering pundits' opinions; 4) government officials presenting political plans and/or policies; 5) representatives of organizations presenting testimony or policy.

66 My mother has a rare disease and is in pain every single day of her life. I think that it [marijuana] is safer
than some of the drugs that doctors want her to take
. . . all those man-made drugs are more harmful then
weed. She would be more likely to get addicted to
those pain medicines and it would be worse for her. 99

—Desiray, "Readers Comments: Medical Marijuana," ProCon.org, January 27, 2011. www.procon.org.

Desiray is among the many Americans who favors the use of marijuana for medical purposes.

66 The reality is that few if any therapeutic or psychoactive substances possess a safety profile comparable to
cannabis. 99

—Paul Armentano, "Marijuana Use Seldom Associated with Emergency Room Visits, First-Ever National Study Says,"
AlterNet, July 20, 2010. http://blogs.alternet.org.

Armentano is the deputy director of NORML.

66 Although evidence against the alleged toxicity [of
marijuana] continues to accumulate, the federal government persists in escalating its war on marijuana
use. 99

—Lester Grinspoon, "Introduction to the Marijuana-Uses Blog by Lester Grinspoon," February 11, 2010. http://
marijuana-uses.com.

An advocate of medical marijuana, Grinspoon is a professor emeritus of psychiatry at Harvard Medical School and a coauthor of the books *Marihuana Reconsid-
ered* and *Marijuana: The Forbidden Medicine*.

66 It will not be a priority to use federal resources to prosecute patients with serious illnesses or their caregivers who are complying with state laws on medical marijuana, but we will not tolerate drug traffickers who hide behind claims of compliance with state law to mask activities that are clearly illegal. 99

—Eric Holder, "Attorney General Announces Formal Medical Marijuana Guidelines," press release, Department of Justice Office of Public Affairs, October 19, 2009.

Holder is the US attorney general.

66 The claim that smoked marijuana is medicinal is a tactic to legalize marijuana for any purpose and to eventually legalize other drugs for personal use. 99

—Drug Free America Foundation, "Marijuana: Questions and Answers," 2008. www.dfaf.org.

The Drug Free America Foundation is a national drug prevention nonprofit committed to opposing efforts that would legalize, decriminalize, or promote illicit drugs, including marijuana.

Should Marijuana Be Legal for Medical Use?

- At the beginning of 2011, **15 states and the District of Columbia** had laws in place to allow marijuana for medicinal purposes.

- In February 2010 *Newsweek* counted **369,634 registered medical marijuana** users in the US states with established programs; California's patient population accounted for roughly **69 percent** of the total.

- A study of AIDS patients conducted by the University of California–San Diego reported **30 percent** reductions in pain among patients who used marijuana.

- In a 2010 AP-CNBC poll, **74 percent** of Americans said marijuana has a real medical benefit for some people.

- In a 2010 ABC News/*Washington Post* poll, **81 percent** of respondents said that doctors should be allowed to prescribe marijuana for medical purposes to treat their patients. This is an increase from its 1997 poll, in which 69 percent agreed that marijuana should be allowed for medical purposes.

- In a 2010 survey conducted by the Pew Research Center, **46 percent** of respondents said that allowing medical marijuana makes it easier for people to get marijuana even if they do not have a real medical need, while **48 percent** said it does not make a difference.

Strong Support for Medical Marijuana

Opinion polls consistently show that most Americans today are in favor of legalizing the use of marijuana for medical purposes under a doctor's guidance. In this 2010 poll taken by ABC News and the *Washington Post*, more than 50 percent of respondents said that medical marijuana should be available to any patient who a doctor thinks might benefit from it. Forty-two percent said that medical marijuana should be made available under more limited care.

Question: If doctors are allowed to prescribe marijuana to patients, should it be limited to patients who are terminally ill and near death; or also allowed for patients who have serious but not fatal illnesses; or should it be allowed for any patient the doctor thinks it could help?

- Terminally Ill
- Seriously Ill
- Any Patient
- Unsure

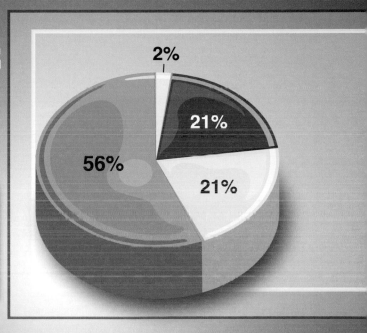

Source: ABC News/*Washington Post* Poll, "Illegal Drugs," January 12–15, 2010. www.pollingreport.com.

- All states with medical marijuana laws limit the **amount of marijuana** and number of **marijuana plants** that a patient can legally have in his or her possession. The maximum amount allowed ranges from a low in Alaska and Montana, which allow just 1 ounce of usable marijuana and 6 plants, to its highest level in Oregon, which allows patients to have 24 ounces and 24 marijuana plants.

Medical Marijuana Is Legal in 15 States

Fifteen states and the District of Columbia have enacted laws to allow the use of cannabis for medical purposes. These have removed state-level criminal penalties for the cultivation, possession, and use of medical marijuana if use has been recommended by a medical doctor. As can be seen from this map, Americans in the West and Northeast appear to be more receptive to the idea of medical marijuana than are those in the Southeast or Midwest.

Source: Congressional Research Service, "Medical Marijuana: Review and Analysis of Federal and State Policies," April 2, 2010. http://medicalmarijuana.procon.org.

- In a Lee Newspapers 2011 public opinion poll of Montana voters, **52 percent** of respondents said they would support repealing the 2004 state law legalizing medical marijuana, and **38 percent** opposed repealing the law; **83 percent** of voters were in favor of stricter regulation and licensing requirements.

- Oregon has the highest per capita rate of medical marijuana patients in the country. In 2009 there were **32,929**; the state population was 3.8 million.

- In 2010 the research firm of Abt Associates estimated that the medical marijuana industry is worth roughly **$10 billion** a year.

- In a 2010 AP/CNBC poll **24 percent** of Americans said they believe the medical marijuana industry will create more jobs, while **57 percent** said it will have no effect.

- CNBC's Special Report *Marijuana & Money* is among news organization reports that the average medical marijuana patient who smokes marijuana uses about **three-quarters** of an ounce a month.

Should Marijuana Be a Legal Substance?

66We have not been able to eradicate the use of hard drugs—cocaine, heroin, meth, etc.—and it would be ridiculous and a waste of public monies to pursue criminally those using marijuana for recreational purposes. My current opinion is that we should follow the Dutch example and legalize its use under rigorous conditions.99

—Ed Koch, former mayor of New York City and a former US congressman representing New York.

66Legalizing marijuana would saddle government with the dual burden of regulating a new legal market while continuing to pay for the negative side effects associated with an underground market whose providers have little economic incentive to disappear.99

—Gil Kerlikowske, director of the Office of National Drug Control Policy.

The debate over whether or not marijuana should be legal has been waged for decades, in the United States and many other countries. Many people believe that marijuana is less harmful than many legal substances, such as alcohol and cigarettes, and that trying to enforce marijuana laws does more harm than good. Opponents of legalizing marijuana say that it is a dangerous substance and that legalizing the drug would increase the number of users—and the associated health risks and dangers for society as a whole.

Marijuana Laws in Other Countries

In no country is it completely legal to produce, sell, or use marijuana, but many countries have relaxed their marijuana laws in recent years. Belgium, Croatia, Germany, Great Britain, Italy, Portugal, Spain, and Switzerland are among the countries that have decriminalized possession of small amounts of marijuana, meaning that users might be subject to confiscation or a fine, but not imprisonment.

In 2001 Portugal made headlines by becoming the first country in the world to decriminalize all street drugs, including marijuana, cocaine, and heroin. People caught possessing these drugs are encouraged to participate in drug rehab programs. Studies suggest that drug-related deaths in Portugal have decreased dramatically since the program was initiated. Moreover, decriminalization has neither increased drug usage among Portuguese citizens nor resulted in "drug tourism," in which people from other countries go to Portugal to do drugs. "Judged by virtually every metric, the Portuguese decriminalization framework has been a resounding success,"[24] concludes a 2009 report of the Cato Institute, a public policy research organization that favors reducing government regulation. The report adds, "Notably, decriminalization has become increasingly popular in Portugal since 2001. Except for some far-right politicians, very few domestic political factions are agitating for a repeal of the 2001 law."[25]

> In no country is it completely legal to produce, sell, or use marijuana, but many countries have relaxed their marijuana laws in recent years.

People on both sides of the issue also have looked to the experience of the Netherlands, which has the most liberal marijuana laws in the world. Some studies show that the percentage of people using marijuana in the Netherlands is higher than in other parts of the world, but marijuana use there remains lower than in the United States. A 2010 study undertaken by the RAND Corporation found that lifetime use "increased consistently and sharply"[26] after the policy shift triggered commercialization, and marijuana use among young adults tripled. "We might expect a similar or worse result here in America's ad-driven culture,"[27] concludes a former staffer at the Office of National Drug Control Policy.

US Marijuana Laws

Current policies on marijuana date from the 1980s, when President Ronald Reagan vowed to "erase the false glamour that surrounds drugs and to brand drugs such as marijuana exactly for what they are—dangerous."[28] Reagan declared a war on drugs, and marijuana became a target of his "Just Say No" antidrug campaign. To spearhead this effort, Reagan created a new cabinet post to coordinate the nation's drug programs. The Office of National Drug Control Policy continues to oversee the president's drug control and prevention efforts.

Penalties for the sale and use of marijuana increased in subsequent years. The Anti-Drug Abuse Act of 1986 established mandatory minimum prison sentences for selling or distributing marijuana. Judges no longer had any leeway in sentencing; the law dictated the sentence without consideration for the circumstances. Another act strengthened asset forfeiture laws, which allowed police to confiscate property and money that may have been obtained by or used in criminal activity. The DEA could seize the assets of suspected marijuana traffickers even if there was insufficient evidence to charge them with a crime. Meanwhile states passed "zero tolerance laws" mandating felony charges for anyone caught with drugs, including marijuana.

> "Some people believe that the costs of enforcing marijuana laws are too high.

Some people believe that the costs of enforcing marijuana laws are too high. Enforcing marijuana laws costs an estimated $10 billion annually and results in the arrest of more than 858,000 individuals per year—more than the total number arrested for all violent crimes. More than 85 percent of Americans charged with marijuana violations are charged with possession only, and almost one-third are under 20 years of age. Advocates of legalization say that being arrested for marijuana ruins the lives of these young people. Some people also argue that arresting occasional marijuana users puts undue strain on the court system and contributes to overcrowding of the nation's prisons.

Leaders of Law Enforcement Against Prohibition are among those who believe that far more harm comes from trying to prohibit marijuana than from the use of marijuana itself. Law Enforcement Against Prohibition argues that legalizing the drug would help wrest control from violent street gangs and even more dangerous

> " **Among the supporters of legalization are people who believe that taxes on the sale of marijuana would be a viable source of state revenues.** "

drug cartels. Legalizing the drug also might eliminate a major source of funds for organized crime and reduce the ability of some to survive.

Decriminalization

A number of states have decriminalized marijuana or reduced penalties for possession of small amounts of the drug. In 1973 Oregon became the first state to decriminalize small amounts of nonmedical marijuana. In October 2010 California, too, decriminalized the drug when Governor Arnold Schwarzenegger signed a bill to make possession of less than 1 ounce (28.35g) of marijuana a civil, rather than a criminal, wrongdoing. This means that possession of marijuana is treated much like a traffic infraction; users face a fine rather than imprisonment. "That's no small matter in a state where arrests for marijuana possession totaled 61,000 last year—roughly triple the number in 1990,"[29] *Huffington Post* columnist Ethan Nadelmann writes of the bill.

While antidrug advocates worry about the impact of reducing penalties for marijuana use, studies suggest that decriminalization has little impact on marijuana use. More than 30 percent of the US population lives in places where marijuana has been decriminalized, and according to government and academic studies, these laws have neither contributed to an increase in marijuana consumption nor negatively impacted adolescent attitudes toward drug use. Surveys undertaken before and after marijuana was decriminalized in Ohio and California, for instance, revealed that marijuana use had increased in both of these states, but that the increase was less than in states that had not decriminalized marijuana. "The available evidence suggests that removal of the prohibition against prohibition itself—decriminalization—does not increase cannabis use," British researchers concluded in a 2001 study: "The fact that Italy and Spain, which have decriminalized possession for all psychoactive drugs, have marijuana use rates comparable to those of neighboring countries provides further support."[30]

Support for Legalization

In the United States support for legalizing marijuana use appears to be at an all-time high. A public opinion poll taken in October 2009 found that almost twice as many Americans support legalizing marijuana today than in the mid-1980s. Among the supporters of legalization are people who believe that taxes on the sale of marijuana would be a viable source of state revenues. In a 2009 Gallup poll, 42 percent of Americans polled said they would support such a measure in their states to raise taxes. In polls conducted from the late 1970s to the mid-1990s, roughly 25 percent of Americans favored legalization for any reason.

Some celebrities have become involved as advocates for legalization. In 1976 reggae singer Peter Tosh wrote a song called "Legalize It" in which he called on the government to repeal laws regulating marijuana. Country star Willie Nelson, who has admitted to being a longtime marijuana smoker, has spoken out for legalization and chose a picture of marijuana leaves for the cover of his 2005 *Countryman* album. Nelson has been arrested several times for drug possession, including a felony charge in November 2010.

Different sectors of the American public feel differently about making marijuana legal. Comparing the results of recent Gallup polls shows growing support for legalization among women, younger Americans, Democrats, moderates, and liberals. In a 2009 Gallup poll, half of those polled under 50 years of age said that marijuana should be legal, while just 28 percent of senior citizens favored legalization.

Regionally, support has grown the most in the West and Midwest, and in some states it approaches or tops 50 percent. This has spurred a few states to put the issue of legalization to the voters. In 2010 ballot initiatives were included on the ballot in California, Oregon, Arizona, and South Dakota.

On the Ballot

People on both sides of the issue hotly debated and carefully followed the debate that ensued when states put the issue to vote, particularly in the large state of California, which had led the way in legalizing medical marijuana. Proposition 19, also known as the Regulate, Control and Tax Cannabis Act of 2010, proposed to allow Californians 21 years or older "to possess, cultivate, or transport marijuana for personal use"[31] and permitted local governments to regulate and tax the sale of marijuana.

Leading up to the election held on November 3, 2010, people on opposite sides of the issue squared off. Proponents of Proposition 19 estimated said it would save the state and California's local governments tens of millions of dollars each year on the costs of arresting and incarcerating marijuana offenders. California also proposed taxes on the sale of the drug, which could have generated millions more in revenues for the state and its localities. Analysts disagreed widely about the implications on the government's budget and the impact on demand and consumption.

The RAND Corporation, an independent think tank, concluded that it was nearly impossible to estimate the impact of legalization on the public budget. The authors of the RAND paper also concluded, "Consumption will increase, but it is unclear how much."[32] Opponents of legalization say that even a small increase in marijuana use is counterproductive and could lead to significant costs to society.

> **Opponents of legalization say that even a small increase in marijuana use is counterproductive and could lead to significant costs to society.**

California voters narrowly defeated Proposition 19 by a margin of just 53.5 percent to 46.5 percent of voters. Experts point out that the margin of victory was slim, however. Experts expect that the issue is likely to be put to voters again in upcoming elections in California and other states.

Marijuana and Crime

One of the arguments against legalization of marijuana is that drug use has an adverse impact not only on the individual user but on society as a whole. The Substance Abuse and Mental Health Services Administration says that marijuana use among young people contributes to delinquent behavior, such as fighting, stealing, and selling illegal drugs. The Substance Abuse and Mental Health Services Administration also reports that these delinquent behaviors increase with the frequency of marijuana use.

After alcohol, marijuana is the next most prevalent substance found in impaired drivers, and there is growing evidence that marijuana use reduces one's ability to drive and increases the risk of car accidents. While the greatest impairment occurs when marijuana is used in conjunction with alcohol, there is increasing evidence that marijuana alone may contribute to thousands of automobile accidents a year. Experts explain that accidents may be a direct result of reduced functioning in the areas of attention, reaction time, and motor control and coordination associated with THC.

Impact of Legalization on Society

Using marijuana is against the law, and some Americans believe that it merits tough sanctions. Others believe that putting people in jail for possessing small amounts of marijuana is a waste of government time and money. As jails and courthouses become crowded with marijuana users, there is less room for more dangerous criminals.

Many people believe that, given the relative harmlessness of marijuana, law enforcement efforts represent a waste of government money and that attention should be refocused on more dangerous drugs. Some Americans believe that legalizing marijuana would help address some of the problems that currently stem from its use by providing regulatory oversight and providing a safe legal source for consumers. In addition, requiring labels on marijuana would help consumers know the level of THC and other ingredients, making the drug safer. Supporters speculate that legalization might encourage users who want to stop to seek treatment.

Some advocates of legalization point to the fact that laws have been largely ineffective in stopping the use of the drug. Despite laws dating back almost 100 years, marijuana remains the most widely used drug in

America. Legalization advocates argue that the money spent trying to enforce drug laws would be better spent on education and other prevention efforts targeting at-risk populations.

The debate over whether marijuana should be a legal substance continues in the halls of Congress, state legislatures, and city halls. Given the strong feelings on both sides of the issue and the mixed messages coming from medical science, widespread agreement is unlikely anytime soon.

Primary Source Quotes*

Should Marijuana Be a Legal Substance?

66 [W]e no longer need police to waste time on marijuana possession. We can safely predict that removing law enforcement from California's marijuana policy would not cause more use. 99

—Jesse Levine, "A Letter to the Undecided: Prop 19," *Huffington Post*, November 1, 2010, www.huffingtonpost.com.

Jesse Levine is an associate researcher with the Marijuana Arrest Research Project.

66 Legalizing marijuana would increase use of the drug and, consequently, the harm it causes, thus adding to the burden on the criminal justice system. 99

—Office of National Drug Control Policy "Marijuana Legalization: A Bad Idea," October 2010, www. whitehousedrugpolicy.gov.

The ONDCP is the White House office responsible for the nation's drug policies.

* Editor's Note: While the definition of a primary source can be narrowly or broadly defined, for the purposes of Compact Research, a primary source consists of: 1) results of original research presented by an organization or researcher; 2) eyewitness accounts of events, personal experience, or work experience; 3) first-person editorials offering pundits' opinions; 4) government officials presenting political plans and/or policies; 5) representatives of organizations presenting testimony or policy.

Primary Source Quotes

66 Drug policymakers in the Portuguese government are virtually unanimous in their belief that decriminalization has enabled a far more effective approach to managing Portugal's addiction problems and other drug-related afflictions. 99

—Glenn Greenwald, *Drug Decriminalization in Portugal: Lessons for Creating Fair and Successful Drug Policies.* Washington, DC: Cato Institute, 2009.

Greenwald is a contributing writer to *Salon.*

66 If we legalized and taxed drug sales, we could actually create new revenue in addition to the money we'd save from ending the cruel policy of arresting users. 99

—Jack Cole, "New FBI Numbers Show Failure of War on Drugs," press release, September 14, 2009. www.leap.cc.

Cole is a retired undercover narcotics detective who now heads the group Law Enforcement Against Prohibition.

66 The revenue gained through a regulated market will never keep pace with the financial and social cost of making this drug [marijuana] more accessible. 99

—R. Gil Kerlikowski, Annotated Remarks to California Police Chiefs Association, March 4, 2010, http://ondcp.gov.

Kerlikowske is the director of the Office of National Drug Control Policy.

66 Contrary to the beliefs of those who advocate the legalization of marijuana, the current balanced, restrictive, and bipartisan drug policies of the United States are working reasonably well and they have contributed to reductions in the rate of marijuana use in our nation. 99

—Robert L. DuPont, "Why We Should Not Legalize Marijuana," *CNBC Marijuana & Money*, April 20, 2010. www.cnbc.com.

A staunch advocate of drug prevention and treatment, DuPont was the first director of the National Institute on Drug Abuse and served as the White House Drug Chief from 1973 to 1978.

66 The debate over [marijuana] legalization should be about more than monetary impacts. . . . The issue of drug prohibition is part of a much bigger picture, one which depends upon our fundamental views on the extent to which the government should have a say over individual choices. 99

—Katherine Waldock, "Drug Legalization—a Windfall for State Budgets," *Huffington Post*, September 29, 2010. www.huffingtonpost.com.

Waldock is a doctoral candidate at New York University's Stern School of Business and a coauthor of the Cato Institute's 2010 study, "The Budgetary Impact of Ending Drug Prohibition."

66 The debate is shifting from whether marijuana should be legalized to how. 99

—Ethan Nadelmann, "Marijuana Legalization: Not If, but When," *Huffington Post*, November 3, 2010. www.huffingtonpost.com.

Nadelmann is the founder and executive director of the Drug Policy Alliance.

Facts and Illustrations

Should Marijuana Be a Legal Substance?

- More than **30 percent** of Americans live in states where marijuana has been decriminalized.

- In an ongoing CNBC poll at Marijuana Inc., **96 percent** of respondents say they advocate the decriminalization of marijuana use.

- A poll conducted by Gallup in the fall of 2010 concluded that **46 percent** of Americans were in favor of legalizing marijuana, compared with just **50 percent** who opposed legalization. This is the highest approval rating since the poll began in the late 1960s.

- In a 2010 Associated Press/CNBC poll, **43 percent** of respondents believed the regulations on marijuana should be stricter than those for alcohol; **44 percent** said they should be the same; and **12 percent** believed marijuana regulations should be less strict than those for alcohol.

- In a 2010 Gallup poll, **50 percent** of Americans under 50 years of age polled said that marijuana should be legal, while just **28 percent** of senior citizens favored legalization.

- A 2010 study undertaken by the Cato Institute estimates that legalizing marijuana would save the government **$8.7 billion** currently spent on law enforcement and accrue an additional $8.7 billion in tax revenues.

Support for Legalization Grows

Opinion polls show that more Americans today are in favor of making marijuana legal than ever before. In an October 2010 poll conducted by Gallup, 46 percent of respondents said they believe marijuana should be made legal. This compares with roughly 25 percent of Americans who favored legalization from the late 1970s to the mid-1990s. As shown in this chart of past Gallup polls, acceptance of marijuana legalization has been growing for more than a decade.

Question: Do you think the use of marijuana should be made legal, or not?

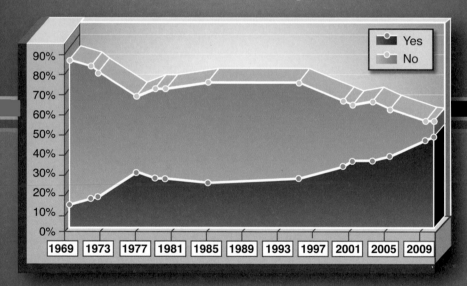

Source: Gallup, "New Height of 46% of Americans Support Legalizing Marijuana," October 28, 2010. www.gallup.com.

- In a 2010 Associated Press/CNBC poll, **46 percent** of respondents said that making marijuana legal would "mostly harm" the health of Americans, and **39 percent** said they believed that legalization would lead people to use more serious drugs such as heroin and cocaine.

The Decriminalization and Relaxation of Marijuana Laws

While no state has legalized marijuana, as of 2011, 13 states have passed laws decriminalizing marijuana. The laws vary, but decriminalization usually means that possession of a small amount of marijuana is treated much like a minor traffic violation; the person convicted does not risk prison time or a criminal record. An increasing number of states also have conditional release programs, which offer people caught using marijuana the option of probation—typically with a requirement that they complete a drug treatment program—rather than going to trial. Some states that have decriminalized marijuana also have conditional release programs. Often, these programs are for possession of amounts of marijuana that are slightly higher than that allowed under the decriminalization law.

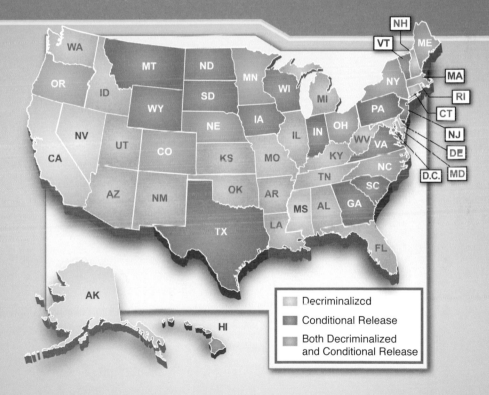

Legend:
- Decriminalized
- Conditional Release
- Both Decriminalized and Conditional Release

Source: NORML, "State by State Laws," January 2, 2011. www.norml.com.

- Statistics from the FBI Uniform Crime Report show an increase in the percentage of drug arrests that are for marijuana over the last decade, accounting for **51.6 percent** in 2009 compared to **30 percent** in 1999.

Marijuana Versus Alcohol

Many people believe that marijuana is safer than many legal substances, including alcohol. A 2010 poll showed that almost half of Americans—45 percent—believed that marijuana should be regulated just like alcohol, while almost the same percent think the laws for marijuana should be more strict than alcohol laws.

Those who favor legalizing marijuana think that:

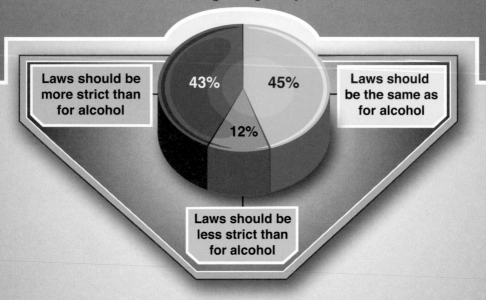

Laws should be more strict than for alcohol — 43%

Laws should be the same as for alcohol — 45%

Laws should be less strict than for alcohol — 12%

Source: GfK Roper Public Affairs & Media, "AP-CNBC Poll", April 7–12, 2010. http://www.ap-gfkpoll.com.

- In a 2010 Associated Press/CNBC poll, **45 percent** of respondents said the cost of enforcing marijuana laws is too high; **48 percent** said the cost was acceptable.

- In a Gallup poll conducted in the fall of 2009, **42 percent** of respondents said they would support a proposal legalizing marijuana and then taxing its sale as a way of raising money for state governments.

- A 2010 study conducted by the RAND Corporation estimated that legalizing marijuana would cause the price of the drug to drop by **80 to 90 percent**, which in turn would cause consumption to rise.

How Effective Are Efforts to Prevent Marijuana Use?

> **Reducing marijuana use is essential to improving the nation's health, education, and productivity.**
>
> —Robert L. DuPont was the first director of the National Institute on Drug Abuse and served as the White House Drug Chief from 1973 to 1978.

> **The Obama Administration, together with Federal partners and State and local officials, is working to reduce the use of marijuana and other illicit drugs through development of strategies that more fully integrate the principles of prevention, treatment, and recovery.**
>
> —Office of National Drug Control Policy, the White House office responsible for drug policy.

U nlike many illegal drugs, marijuana has been embraced by a wide variety of people, including many high-profile and prominent musicians, athletes, and even politicians, lending marijuana credibility as a harmless recreational drug. Americans have used marijuana for recreational purposes since the early 1800s. Nineteenth-century cities boasted hashish parlors, where wealthy patrons smoked hashish from elaborate pipes known as hookahs. During the 1920s marijuana became associated with jazz; from New Orleans to New York City, jazz clubs sprang up, in which players and listeners alike consumed marijuana. The author of an article titled "Marijuana—the First Twelve Thousand Years" explains: "Unlike booze, which dulled and incapacitated, marihuana enabled musicians whose job required them to play long into the night to forget their exhaustion. Moreover, the drug seemed to make their music sound more imaginative and unique, at least to those who played and listened to it while under its sensorial influence."[33]

Jazz may have been the first musical genre to be associated with marijuana, but it was not the last. Bob Marley, a Jamaican who introduced reggae to the world in the 1970s, was a dedicated smoker of what the Jamaicans called "ganja," and some people believe that Marley's marijuana use may have contributed to the brain cancer that killed him in 1981. Singers Mick Jagger, Whitney Houston, James Brown, David Lee Roth, Snoop Dogg, and George Michael all have been arrested more recently on charges of possession of marijuana.

> " Unlike many illegal drugs, marijuana has been embraced by a wide variety of people, including many high-profile and prominent musicians, athletes, and even politicians, lending marijuana credibility as a harmless recreational drug. "

Athletes, too, have been caught using marijuana. In 2003 Ricky Williams, winner of the 1998 Heisman Trophy as the best college football player, received a $650,000 fine and a four-game suspension from the Miami Dolphins after testing positive for marijuana. Michael Phelps, who won gold medal records for swimming at the 2008 Olympic Games, was suspended from competition for three months after being caught smoking marijuana. Phelps also lost a major sponsorship deal with Kellogg.

A number of other famous Americans have admitted to marijuana use. During the 1992 presidential campaign, Bill Clinton admitted to smoking marijuana, but he added a caveat about his experience: "When I was in England, I experimented with marijuana a time or two, and I didn't like it, and didn't inhale; and never tried it again."[34] Barack Obama's admission to marijuana use was more forthright than Clinton's. "When

I was a kid I inhaled frequently," he told reporters during his 2008 presidential campaign. "That was the point."[35]

Law Enforcement Strategies

A critical aspect of efforts to prevent the spread of marijuana use, say antidrug advocates and law enforcement experts, is to stop the supply of marijuana, both within and beyond US borders. To this end, the DEA has stepped up efforts to catch smugglers as they cross into the United States. In 2009 the DEA initiated a Southwest Border Counternarcotics Strategy, in which federal, state, and local law enforcement agencies work together to identify and dismantle Mexican drug cartels. The DEA points to several successes in this attack. For instance, on June 10, 2010, 2,266 people were arrested on drug-related charges in the United States, as part of a sting called Project Deliverance. A total of 74.1 tons (67.2 metric tons) of illegal drugs was seized, including 69 tons (62.6 metric tons) of marijuana.

Law enforcement agencies have also sought to eradicate marijuana plants grown within the United States. The DEA's Cannabis Eradication/Suppression Program provides funding and support to state and local law enforcement agencies, which use helicopters, trucks, and off-road vehicles to identify marijuana fields.

Some people believe that such attempts are fruitless. For every marijuana plant destroyed, thousands more continue to thrive. In Appalachia, where the poverty rate is far above the national average, many people may see growing marijuana as the best—or only—way to make a living. Where the odds of getting caught are minimal and punishment minimal, marijuana growers may be willing to take the risk.

Alternatives to Jail Time

The arrest and sentencing of Americans for the possesion of small amounts of marijuana has long been controversial. As with supply, many people believe that trying to curb demand by arresting users is fruitless. Statistics show that sentencing also is problematic. Arrests have increased fourfold since the early 1990s, but the risk of being arrested for marijuana possession and use is minimal: there is just 1 arrest for every 11,000 to 12,000 joints consumed.

Some states have implemented new approaches in prosecuting and sentencing marijuana cases. For instance, prearrest diversion programs have been piloted in High Point, North Carolina; Seattle, Washington; and Providence, Rhode Island. These programs threaten small-time marijuana dealers and users with jail time but also offer treatment programs and other resources to help them change their lives. In an interview on National Public Radio, R. Gil Kerlikowske explained the goal of such prearrest diversion programs:

> We know young people get into trouble with drugs. We know that some of them are dealing drugs. And we know that if we make the arrest that quite often there is a stigma attached to that that is pretty difficult for them to get out from under. And so this pre-arrest diversion program has great promise because it gives young people the chance to get out from under what they've done without an arrest record, but it also gives them an opportunity if they need treatment programs, if they need literacy, if they need vocational training. And it all has the sanction of the criminal justice system behind it, which actually quite often is a motivator to keep out of trouble.[36]

Piloted more than 20 years ago into the criminal justice system, drug courts also have been shown to be effective in changing behavior of young people who have gotten in trouble with the law. Drug courts require arrestees to keep in contact with the sentencing judge and submit to random drug tests.

People on probation for marijuana use also are often required to participate in drug treatment. In fact, more than half of the people seeking treatment for marijuana are referred to treatment through the criminal justice system.

Education and Prevention

Research indicates that drug use is linked to the perception of risk. Anti-drug campaigns that convince young people of the serious health dangers of marijuana use are most likely to have an impact. Often these programs are incorporated into the health curricula of schools, starting with early elementary grades. Many programs have built off of the success and lessons learned by early pioneers such as the Drug Awareness Resistance

Education (D.A.R.E.) program, a national program begun in 1983. In the D.A.R.E. model, police officers partner with public schools to educate young people about the dangers of drugs such as marijuana.

Drug prevention programs such as D.A.R.E. have met with mixed results. Some researchers caution that many such programs have little impact on behavior. In its review of numerous studies undertaken on the effectiveness of D.A.R.E., the Government Accounting Office found that the program was largely ineffective. In 2011, Knox County, Tennessee, discontinued the D.A.R.E. program after 25 years, citing the lack of clear results.

> **A critical aspect of prevention, say experts, is to stop the supply of marijuana, both within and beyond US borders.**

The best programs, say experts, are those that combine information about the health risks associated with marijuana use with life skills training that teaches students how to deal with stress and peer pressure. Project ALERT and Life Skills Training—both examples of drug prevention programs that include strong social learning components—have each been found to reduce marijuana use. Research suggests that the effectiveness of these programs lessens over time, however.

Programs facilitated by individuals other than teachers may yield stronger effects. Teachers often lack credibility; in many cases, students know more—or think they know more –about marijuana than teachers do. In school-based programs, peers often play a particularly important role as mentors or role models. Studies suggest that peer programs are consistently more successful in curtailing marijuana use.

Research also shows that school-based antidrug programs can have a greater impact when they are combined with media and community programs. Media campaigns reinforce school-based prevention programs by reaching youth through popular television shows, Internet sites, magazines, and films. Antidrug media campaigns include a variety of media to communicate the dangers of drug use, including public service announcements, posters and print advertisements, brochures on the dangers of drug abuse, web-based testimonials, and the like.

Community-Based Programs

Effective programs often include a community focus. For instance, the National Youth Anti-Drug Media Campaign's "Above the Influence" program delivers drug prevention messages at the national level and through more targeted efforts at the local community level. In 2010 the Office of National Drug Control Policy retooled this program to target the greatest risks for young people, namely, alcohol and marijuana abuse.

The Office of National Drug Control Policy also oversees the Drug Free Communities program, which was funded initially by Congress in 1997 in recognition of the fact that local problems need local solutions. Drug Free Communities provides the funding necessary for communities to identify and respond to local substance abuse problems.

Intervention and Drug Testing

Many antidrug advocates believe that early intervention and ongoing monitoring are critical aspects of a prevention program. Some state and local governments require routine, random drug testing on people on probation for drug use or other crimes. Drug tests also are often required for police officers, prison guards, and military personnel, as well as professional athletes. An increasing number of high school and college sports programs require athletes to take drug tests; while the purpose of such testing is often to detect performance-enhancing drugs, the tests sometimes screen athletes for marijuana as well. Antidrug advocates applaud these efforts and many recommend that random drug tests should be performed on students wishing to participate in other extracurricular activities as well.

> " Research indicates that drug use is linked to the perception of risk. "

Drug tests to detect marijuana are very accurate. Among frequent users, traces of marijuana will show up in the user's urine for as long as 15 weeks following its use. The drug can also be detected in hair follicles. Studies show that drug tests can be effective as a prevention tool. Tests may be particularly helpful in ensuring that people in court-mandated treatment programs stay drug free.

Treatment Programs

A recent phenomenon in both the United States and other Western countries is a substantial increase in the number of individuals seeking treatment for marijuana abuse or dependence. Nationally, marijuana now accounts for the largest number of treatment episodes (excluding alcohol)—about 322,000 in 2008, compared with 92,500 in 1992. In that period the share of treatment admissions for which marijuana was the primary drug grew from about 6 percent with 17 percent.

Experts once believed that marijuana users did not need treatment, because marijuana was not physically addictive, but today most agree that the psychological dependence on marijuana may make it difficult to quit without support. Behavioral therapy is often at the cornerstone of marijuana treatment programs. Such therapy often includes motivational techniques intended to help people take ownership of their problem and treatment.

Traditional therapy for marijuana addicts often includes a discussion or support group led by a psychologist or other therapist. Such group therapy is designed to provide a safe forum for participants to talk about their drug problems and what they want to do about them. These group therapy sessions are usually most effective when combined with skill-based training that helps marijuana users recognize the situations in which they use drugs (such as being depressed, lonely, or stressed) and then working with them to develop plans and build coping skills to use in these situations. Methods may include relaxation exercises, imaging, or role-playing.

> " Experts once believed that marijuana users did not need treatment, because marijuana was not physically addictive, but today most agree that the psycho logical dependence on marijuana may make it difficult to quit without support. "

Treatment programs also address some of the physical symptoms associated with sudden cessation of marijuana. Long-term marijuana users who are trying to stop using the drug report symptoms such as irritability, sleeplessness, decreased appetite, anxiety, and drug craving, all of which make it difficult to quit. These symptoms often peak between 48 and 72 hours from the last use and can last for 1 or 2 weeks. If the drug use is halted abruptly, there is a higher risk of experiencing severe withdrawal symptoms, so some treatment programs advocate gradual reduction of use.

The success rates of treatment programs vary widely. Not surprisingly, treatment is most effective when people wanted to stop using for intrinsic reasons; for instance, when they believed marijuana was contributing to confusion, memory loss, or a lack of self-confidence. Treatment programs also tend to be more effective among participants who have supportive family and friends and who do not abuse alcohol or other drugs.

Into the Future

There is no one strategy for reducing the use of marijuana. Given the wide range of users, prevention measures will have to reach far and wide into the population. Effective education and prevention programs will need to reach teens when they are first tempted to take marijuana. These programs will also need to convince entertainers and other role models that it is time to give the drugs up. Given the growing support for legalization and for medical marijuana, the weed is likely to continue to be part of American life for many years to come.

How Effective Are Efforts to Prevent Marijuana Use?

66 **Evidence shows that peer programs are one of the most effective strategies to prevent substance abuse.** 99

—Judith A. Tindall and David R. Black, *Peer Programs: An In-Depth Look at Peer Programs Planning, Implementation, and Administration*. New York: Routledge, 2009, p. 35.

Tindall is president of the Psychological Network, Inc., a treatment group in St. Charles, Missouri; Black is an educational psychologist and writer.

66 **[C]urrent drug education programs are likely to be ineffective. These programs over-emphasize peer pressure as being an external force. They encourage individuals to be strong and resist the influences of their peer group, thus promoting isolation rather than connectedness.** 99

—Dan Reist, "Rethinking Drug Education," *Visions: BC/s Mental Health and Addictions Journal,* 2009. http://heretohelp.bc.ca.

Reist is the Director of the Communication and Resource Unit for the Centre for Addictions Research of BC at the University of Victoria.

Bracketed quotes indicate conflicting positions.

* Editor's Note: While the definition of a primary source can be narrowly or broadly defined, for the purposes of Compact Research, a primary source consists of: 1) results of original research presented by an organization or researcher; 2) eyewitness accounts of events, personal experience, or work experience; 3) first-person editorials offering pundits' opinions; 4) government officials presenting political plans and/or policies; 5) representatives of organizations presenting testimony or policy.

Primary Source Quotes

66 The goal of 'disrupting supply' has been proved farcical. Drugs are as widely available as ever. 99

—Tim Lynch, "Drug Czar Should Go," *Washington Times*, February 6, 2010. www.washingtontimes.com.

Lynch is the director of the Cato Institute's Project on Criminal Justice.

66 The basic method used formerly in drug education has been the 'scare tactic' approach. This was an attempt to scare youth away from drugs. It never worked and in many cases perpetuated drug use by presenting information that was easily discredited. 99

—Narconon International, "Drug Education Programs," 2011. www.narconon.org.

The Narconon program is a worldwide network of over 120 drug prevention and drug-free social education rehabilitation centers.

66 Experience has shown that some of the most innovative and effective approaches to dealing with adolescent drug and alcohol problems begins at the community level. 99

—The Partnership at DrugFree.org, "Community Education," 2011. www.drugfree.org.

The Partnership at Drugfree.org is a nonprofit organization that helps parents prevent, intervene in, and find treatment for drug and alcohol use by their children.

66 The best solution is to reach young people with effective, fact-based drug education—before they start experimenting with drugs. Tweens, teens and young adults who know the facts about drugs are much less likely to start using them. 99

—Foundation for a Drug-Free World, "Effective Drug Education Tools for All Teachers and Educators," 2011. www.drugfreeworld.org.

The Foundation is a nonprofit corporation dedicated to the prevention of drug use.

"Although many drug education programs have increased knowledge and produced significant attitude changes, traditional drug education programs have not proved to be effective. Information alone does not alter behavior."

Raymond Goldberg, *Drugs Across the Spectrum*. Belmont, CA: Wadsworth, 2010, p. 324.

Goldberg is the Dean of Health Sciences at Vance-Granville Community College in North Carolina.

"Governments around the world have given more funding for drug education over the last decade to help young people learn the skills to remain drug free. The best of these programs might stop or delay the onset of drug use in a small percentage of students under perfect conditions. Programs delivered in normal classrooms have not shown effectiveness."

—Dan Reist, "Rethinking Drug Education," *Visions: BC's Mental Health and Addictions Journal*, 2009. http://heretohelp.bc.ca.

Reist is the Director of the Communication and Resource Unit for the Centre for Addictions Research of BC at the University of Victoria.

"So many times I tried to stop [marijuana use] on my own—saying to myself, I can do this! But every single time I found myself right back where I was to begin with. . . . It wasn't until I was basically forced to get help that I was able to actually quit."

—Glitter, The Sober Recovery Community, September 13, 2010. www.soberrecovery.com.

Glitter, a daily marijuana smoker, posted a message about her struggle to quit on an Internet support group site.

How Effective Are Efforts to Prevent Marijuana Use?

- A 2009 report of the Substance Abuse and Mental Health Service Administration shows that **69 percent** of Americans in households with children and **59 percent** in households without children believe that marijuana use can be prevented.

- Despite prevention efforts, the 2010 National Survey on Drug Use and Health shows that roughly **11.3 percent** of adult Americans have used marijuana in the past year.

- Efforts to reduce the supply of marijuana have had little effect; NORML estimates that **9 million** marijuana plants are grown in the United States each year, earning cultivators $15 billion.

- In the 2009 Monitoring the Future Study, nearly **50 percent** of youths aged 12 to 17 said that it would be "fairly easy" or "very easy" for them to obtain marijuana if they wanted it.

- According to the DEA, more than **4 million** marijuana plants are eradicated annually from US public lands. Some of this marijuana is grown by Mexican drug cartels.

- Oklahoma, Florida, and Louisiana have the toughest marijuana laws in the country. In Oklahoma the fine for possession can be as much as **$10,000**, the highest in the country.

Changing Perception of Marijuana Risks

Studies show that young people today see much less risk in occasional marijuana use than did their peers of 20 years ago. Drug-prevention experts are alarmed by this change in attitude because perception of risk is thought to be a deciding factor for teens contemplating trying marijuana. Experts say that educating young people about the risks of marijuana is a key tool for reducing use.

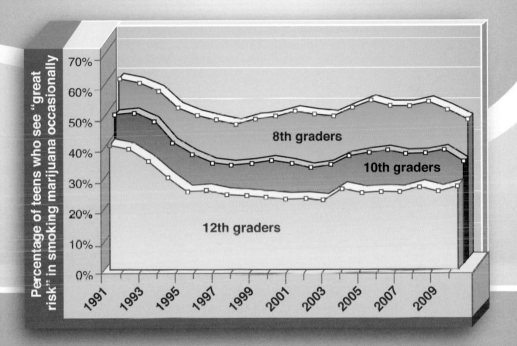

Source: University of Michigan, The Monitoring the Future study, 2009, Tables 11–13, http://monitoringthefuture.org.

- The 2010 National Survey on Drug Use and Health shows that, on an average day, **563,182** teens aged 12 to 17 use marijuana. This compares with **508,329** in this age group who use alcohol and just **80,797** who use all other drugs combined.

Parental Disapproval Plays a Role in Teen Marijuana Use

In the 2009 National Survey of Drug Use and Health, over 90 percent of teens reported that their parents would strongly disapprove of their trying marijuana or hashish once or twice. As shown in the figure below, current marijuana use was much less prevalent among youths who perceived strong parental disapproval for trying marijuana or hashish once or twice than for those who did not.

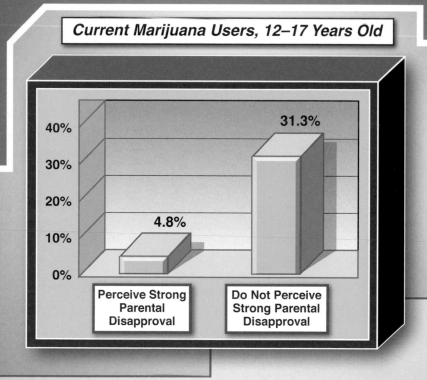

Current Marijuana Users, 12–17 Years Old

Source: SAMHSA, *Results from the 2009 National Survey on Drug Use and Health*, 2009. http://oas.samhsa.gov.

- In the 2009 National Household Survey on Drug Abuse, just **4.8 percent** of teen marijuana users said their parents have expressed strong disapproval of marijuana use, whereas **34.3 percent** of marijuana users said their parents do not strongly disapprove.

Teens Say Marijuana Is Easy to Get

Experts say that keeping marijuana out of the hands of young people is critical to prevention but in most areas marijuana is widely available to teens who want it. As shown from this graph, more than four of every five high school seniors and two of every five eighth-graders say it would be easy to get marijuana if they wanted it. Although this is down slightly from the mid-to late-1990s, it is not significantly lower than when the study began in 1992.

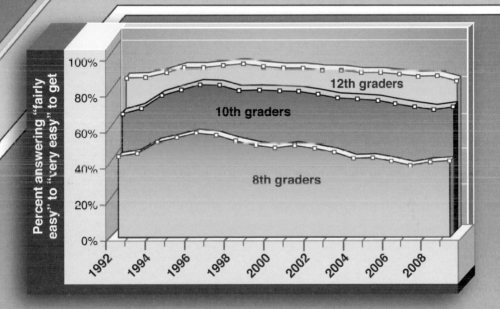

Question: How difficult do you think it would be for you to get marijuana?

Percent answering "fairly easy" to "very easy" to get

12th graders

10th graders

8th graders

Source: University of Michigan, The Monitoring the Future study, 2009, Tables 11–13, http://monitoringthefuture.org.

- According to the Substance Abuse and Mental Health Services Administration, fewer than **one-fifth** of Americans say they know anyone in recovery from addiction to marijuana. More than twice as many Americans say they know someone in recovery from addiction to alcohol.

Key People and Advocacy Groups

Jack Cole: After retiring from a 26-year career with the New Jersey State Police, 14 of which were spent as an undercover narcotics officer, Cole served as the first executive director of Law Enforcement Against Prohibition. Cole is an outspoken critic of current federal drug policy, arguing that it is needlessly destroying the lives of young people and corrupting our police.

Drug Free America Foundation (DFAF): The DFAF is a national drug prevention nonprofit organization committed to opposing efforts that would legalize, decriminalize, or promote illicit drugs, including marijuana.

Drug Policy Alliance (DPA): The DPA lobbies for drug reform policy that is grounded in science, compassion, health, and human rights and seeks alternatives to the US government's failed war on drugs.

Robert L. DuPont: DuPont was the first director of the National Institute on Drug Abuse and served as the White House Drug Chief from 1973 to 1978. He is a staunch advocate of drug prevention and treatment and an outspoken critic of proposals to legalize marijuana for any purpose.

Mitch Earleywine: An associate professor of psychology at the State University of New York at Albany, Earleywine is an advocate of the reform of marijuana laws, particularly for medical marijuana. He is also the author of several books, including *Parents' Guide to Marijuana*, which provides factual information to help parents talk to their children about drug use.

Green Aid: The Medical Marijuana Legal Defense and Education Fund: This nonprofit activist organization seeks reform of marijuana laws through legal means.

R. Gil Kerlikowske: The director of the Office of National Drug Control Policy, Kerlikowske maintains that decriminalizing or legalizing marijuana for any purpose would have a negative impact on public health and give the wrong message to kids.

Law Enforcement Against Prohibition (LEAP): LEAP is an organization of former law enforcement and criminal justice professionals who are speaking out about the failures of our existing drug policies. The mission of LEAP is to reduce the multitude of harms resulting from fighting the war on drugs and to lessen the incidence of death, disease, crime, and addiction by ultimately ending drug prohibition.

Marijuana Policy Project (MPP): The MPP is the leading national sponsor of ballot initiatives and lobbying campaigns to reform marijuana laws; its main focus is on removing criminal penalties for marijuana use, with a particular emphasis on making marijuana medically available to seriously ill people who have the approval of their doctors.

Willie Nelson: This country music superstar and self-professed habitual marijuana user has long used his fame to advocate legalization of marijuana.

NORML (National Organization for the Reform of Marijuana Laws): This Washington-based group lobbies for the support of liberalizing laws that govern marijuana use in America. The group has compiled numerous studies showing the benefits of marijuana for medicinal purposes.

Angel Raich: Raich, a mother of two who suffers from an inoperable brain tumor, is a spokesperson for medical marijuana and has sued the government to allow her to use marijuana to treat the symptoms of her illness.

StoptheDrugWar.org: Founded in 1993, StoptheDrugWar.org calls for replacing drug prohibition with a framework in which drugs can be regulated and controlled instead.

Chronology

2737 BC
The first written record of the use of cannabis for medicine is made in China; among the illnesses treated with cannabis are constipation, gout, malaria, rheumatism, and absentmindedness.

1621
In his book *The Anatomy of Melancholy*, English clergyman Robert Burton recommends cannabis as a treatment for depression.

1915
Utah passes the first state law prohibiting the use of marijuana; California and Texas soon follow suit.

1880s
Hashish parlors are present in every major American city; there are 500 in New York City alone.

1936
US government filmmakers release *Reefer Madness*, a propaganda film that exaggerates the dangers of marijuana use and plays on public fears of drug-addicted teens.

BC   **1600**   **1850**   **1950**

1619
Jamestown Colony, Virginia, enacts the New World's first marijuana legislation: All farmers are required to grow cannabis. Similar laws are passed in Massachusetts in 1631, Connecticut in 1632, and the Chesapeake Colonies in the 1700s.

1914
Congress passes the Harrison Narcotics Act, its first attempt to control the recreational use of drugs. Marijuana is exempt from the law.

1937
The Marijuana Tax Act outlaws cannabis; during hearings a doctor representing the American Medical Association testifies that the law could deny the world a potential medicine.

Late 1600s
Cannabis is used in Africa to restore appetite, to relieve pain, and in the treatment of tetanus, cholera, skin diseases, and a host of other ailments.

1944
The LaGuardia Committee, commissioned by New York mayor Fiorello LaGuardia, concludes that there is no link between cannabis and violence, instead citing the beneficial effects of marijuana.

1964
Raphael Mechoulam of the University of Tel Aviv in Israel isolates delta-9-tetrahydrocannabinol, the primary active ingredient in cannabis, one of at least 60 compounds found in cannabis that have therapeutic value.

1973
Oregon takes the first steps toward decriminalization of cannabis, classifying possession of up to one ounce as a misdemeanor.

1985
The US Food and Drug Administration approves Marinol (dronabinol), a synthetic THC drug, to treat nausea and vomiting associated with chemotherapy and appetite loss in AIDS patients.

1996
California becomes the first state to legalize the use of marijuana for medical purposes when 56 percent of voters approve a ballot initiative allowing the legal use of marijuana under a doctor's supervision.

2001
Canada becomes the first country to pass legislation allowing the use of marijuana for medical purposes.

1960

1985

2010

1970
The Controlled Substances Act categorizes drugs based on abuse and addiction potential compared with their therapeutic value. Marijuana is classified as a Schedule I drug, the category used for drugs that have a high potential for abuse and no currently accepted medical use.

1986
The Anti-Drug Abuse Act reinstates mandatory minimum prison sentences for selling or distributing marijuana.

2005
The US Supreme Court rules in *Gonzales v. Raich* that the federal government has the right to prosecute growers of marijuana even when the growers are using the marijuana for medicinal purposes.

2006
The US Food and Drug Administration issues a statement declaring that smoked marijuana is not medicine.

1978
The Investigational New Drug Compassionate Access Program is passed. Thousands of patients with AIDS, cancer, and other serious illnesses apply to use marijuana under this program, but fewer than 100 are admitted to the program before it is shut down in 1991.

2010
The first cannabis-based prescription medicine, a mouth spray, is introduced in the United Kingdom to treat multiple sclerosis–related spasticity; California's voters narrowly defeat a measure on the ballot to legalize marijuana.

Related Organizations

Americans for Safe Access

1322 Webster St., Suite 208
Oakland, CA 94612
phone: (888) 929-4367
e-mail: info@safeaccessnow.org • website: www.safeaccessnow.org

This is a member-based organization devoted to legislation, education, litigation, and grassroots advocacy for medical marijuana patients and providers.

Common Sense for Drug Policy (CSDP)

1377-C Spencer Ave.
Lancaster, PA 17603
phone: (717) 299-0600 • fax: (717) 393-4953
e-mail: info@csdp.org • website: www.csdp.org

The CSDP is a nonprofit organization dedicated to reforming drug policy and expanding harm reduction. The CSDP disseminates factual information and comments on existing laws, policies, and practices.

Drug Policy Alliance

70 W. Thirty-Sixth St.
New York, NY 10018
phone: (212) 613-8020 • fax: (212) 613-8021
e-mail: nyc@drugpolicy.org • website: www.drugpolicyalliance.com

The Drug Policy Alliance supports and publicizes alternatives to current US policies on illegal drugs, including marijuana.

Foundation for a Drug-Free World

1626 N. Wilcox Ave., Suite 1297
Los Angeles, CA 90028
phone: (888) 668-6378
website: www.drugfreeworld.org

The Foundation for a Drug-Free World is a nonprofit corporation that spearheads a multipronged approach, including public service announcements, educational programs and materials, and web-based outreach, to prevent drug use.

Marijuana Policy Project (MPP)

PO Box 77492
Washington, DC 20013
e-mail: info@mpp.org • website: www.mpp.org

The MPP is the leading national sponsor of ballot initiatives and lobbying campaigns to reform marijuana laws; its main focus is on removing criminal penalties for marijuana use, with a particular emphasis on making marijuana medically available to seriously ill people who have the approval of their doctors.

National Center on Addiction and Substance Abuse (CASA)

633 Third Ave.
New York, NY 10017-6706
phone: (212) 841-5200
website: www.casacolumbia.org

CASA is a nonprofit organization that brings together the professional disciplines needed to study and combat abuse of all substances, including marijuana and other illegal drugs.

National Institute on Drug Abuse (NIDA)

6001 Executive Blvd., Room 5213
Bethesda, MD 20892
phone: (301) 443-1124
e-mail: information@nida.nih.gov • website: www.nida.nih.gov

NIDA is part of the National Institutes of Health, a branch of the US Department of Health and Human Services. It both supports and conducts extensive scientific research on drug abuse and addiction. By disseminating its research findings, NIDA hopes to prevent drug abuse, improve treatment options, and influence public policy.

NORML (National Organization for the Reform of Marijuana Laws)

1600 K St. NW, Suite 501
Washington, DC 20006
phone: (202) 483-5500 • fax: (202) 483-0057
e-mail: norml@norml.org • website: www.norml.org

Founded in 1970, NORML is a public interest group dedicated to marijuana law reform and decriminalization. It offers consumer information, legal guidance, and information on scientific research.

Office of National Drug Control Policy (ONDCP)

PO Box 6000
Rockville, MD 20849-6000
phone: (800) 666-3332 • fax: (301) 519-5212
website: www.whitehousedrugpolicy.gov

The ONDCP was established by the Anti-Drug Abuse Act of 1988 to formulate and implement the nation's drug control program. The goals of the program are to reduce illicit drug use and drug-related trafficking, crime, and violence.

Partnership for a Drug-Free America

405 Lexington Ave., Suite 1601
New York, NY 10174
phone: (212) 922-1560 • fax: (212) 922-1570
website: www.drugfreeamerica.org

The Partnership for a Drug-Free America is a nonprofit organization that works to educate the public, particularly young people, about the dangers of drug abuse. Through extensive media campaigns, the partnership hopes to spread its antidrug message and prevent drug abuse among the nation's youth.

Substance Abuse and Mental Health Services Administration (SAMHSA)

1 Choke Cherry Rd.
Rockville, MD 20857
phone: (877) 726-4727 • fax: (240) 221-4292
website: www.samhsa.gov

This US Department of Health and Human Services administers programs to address substance abuse among Americans and collects and disseminates national data, including the annual National Survey on Drug Use and Health, the Drug Abuse Warning Network, and the Drug and Alcohol Services Information System.

US Drug Enforcement Administration (DEA)

2401 Jefferson Davis Hwy.
Alexandria, VA
phone: (202) 307-1000
website: www.usdoj.gov/dea

The DEA enforces federal laws that prohibit the trafficking of illegal drugs, including marijuana, and assists state and local law enforcement officers in their efforts to stop illegal drug trafficking and abuse.

For Further Research

Books
Steve Fox et al., *Marijuana Is Safer: So Why Are We Driving People to Drink?* White River Junction, VT: Chelsea Green, 2009.

Arthur Gillard, *Marijuana.* Farmington Hills, MI: Greenhaven, 2009.

Margaret J. Goldstein, *Legalizing Drugs: Crime Stopper or Social Risk?* Minneapolis, MN: Twenty-First Century, 2010.

John Geluardi, *Cannabiz: The Explosive Rise of the Medical Marijuana Industry.* Sausalito, CA: PoliPoint, 2010.

Paul Ruschmann, *Legalizing Marijuana.* New York: Chelsea House, 2011.

Julie Holland, *The Pot Book: A Complete Guide to Cannabis.* Rochester, VT: Park Street, 2010.

Periodicals
Jessica Bennett, "Down, but Not Burnt Out," *Newsweek*, November 3, 2010.

Andrew Ferguson, "The United States of Amerijuana," *Time*, November 11, 2010.

Russ Juskalian, "Disjointed," *Newsweek*, November 3, 2010.

Joe Klein, "Why Legalizing Marijuana Makes Sense," *Time*, April 2, 2009.

Jeffrey Kluger, "The Science of Pot," *Time*, November 11, 2010.

Ian Yarett, "Back Story: How High Are You?," *Newsweek*, February 15, 2010.

Internet Sources
CNBC, "Marijuana & Money," special report, 2010. www.cnbc.com/id/36022433.

Mark Eddy, *Medical Marijuana: Review and Analysis of Federal and State Policies.* Washington, DC: Congressional Research Service, April 2, 2010. www.fas.org/sgp/crx/misc./RL33211.PDF.

Frontline, "Busted: America's War on Marijuana," PBS. www.pbs.org/wgbh/pages/frontline/shows/dope.

Zosia Kmietowicz, "Countries Should Consider Legalising Cannabis in Light of Futility of Bans," *BMJ*, October 7, 2010. www.bmj.com/content/341/bmj.c5471.

National Women's Health Information Center, "Smoking and How to Quit: Marijuana," May 19, 2010. www.womenshealth.gov/quit-smoking/otherforms/marijuana.cfm.

NIH News, "Teen Marijuana Use Increases, Especially Among Eighth-Graders," December 14, 2010. www.nih.gov/news/health/dec2010/nida-14.htm.

Robert Preidt, "Early 'Pot' Use May Harm Brain More: Study," Health-Day, November 15, 2010. www.nlm.nih.gov/medlineplus/news/full-story_105570.html.

Websites

Drug Sense (www.drugsense.org). This site provides a comprehensive index of online news clips about marijuana and other drugs.

Drug War Facts (www.drugwarfacts.org). This website provides reliable, up-to-date information pertaining to public health and criminal justice issues.

International Association for Cannabis as Medicine (www.cannabis-med.org). Based in Germany, the association provides abundant information on the results of controlled clinical trials, many of which are posted on this site.

"Marijuana," Medline Plus (www.nlm.nih.gov/medlineplus/marijuana.html#cat57). This site provides links to information about marijuana statistics, news, research, treatment, and related issues for various audiences.

"Medical Marijuana," ProCon.org (http://medicalmarijuana.procon.org). This website provides information about the use of medical marijuana, the issues raised in considering whether marijuana should be legal for medical use, and expert opinions on both sides of the issue.

Schafer Library of Drug Policy (www.druglibrary.org/schaffer). This website provides historical documents, books, and periodicals about the war on drugs.

Source Notes

Overview

1. Jonathan Owen, "Cannabis: An Apology," *Independent*, March 18, 2007. www.independent.co.uk.
2. Mark Eddy, *Medical Marijuana: Review and Analysis of Federal and State Policies*. Washington, DC: Congressional Research Service, April 2, 2010. www.crs.gov.

Is Marijuana a Dangerous Drug?

3. Dale Gieringer, "Marijuana Health Mythology," CA NORML Health Information, March 2005. www.canorml.org.
4. American Cancer Society, "How to Control Your Cancer Risk," April 14, 2009. www.cancer.org.
5. Quoted in Marc Kaufman, "Study Finds No Cancer-Marijuana Connection," *Washington Post*, May 26, 2006. www.washingtonpost.com.
6. Caihua Liang et al., "A Population-Based Case-Control Study of Marijuana Use and Head and Neck Squamous Cell Carcinoma," *Cancer Research Prevention*, August 2009, p. 766. http://cancerpreventionresearch.aacrjournals.org.
7. Alcohol Drug Abuse Resource Center, "Marijuana Addiction." www.addict-help.com/marijuana.asp.
8. Thomas J. O'Connell and Che B. Bou-Matar, "Long-Term Marijuana Users Seeking Medical Cannabis in California (2001–2007)," *Harm Reduction Journal*, November 2007. www.harmreductionjournal.com.
9. O'Connell and Bou-Matar, "Long-Term Marijuana Users Seeking Medical Cannabis in California (2001–2007)."

Should Marijuana Be Legal for Medical Use?

10. *Providence Journal*, Quoted in "Myths About Medical Marijuana," March 26, 2004. www.maps.org.
11. Janet E. Joy, Stanley J. Watson Jr., and John A. Benson Jr., *Marijuana and Medicine: Assessing the Science Base*. Washington, DC: Institute of Medicine of the National Academies, 1999, p.177.
12. Robert L. DuPont, "Marijuana and Medicine: The Need for a Science-Based Approach," testimony submitted to Senate Judicial Proceedings Committee, State of Maryland, March 14, 2007. www.ibhinc.org.
13. American Medical Association, "Report 3 of the Council on Science and Public Health (I-09): Use of Cannabis for Medicinal Purposes," 2009. www.ama-assn.org.
14. DuPont, "Marijuana and Medicine."
15. Drug Free America Foundation, "Marijuana: Questions and Answers," 2008. www.dfaf.org.
16. US Drug Enforcement Administration, "'Medical' Marijuana: The Facts." www.justice.gov.
17. Quoted in J.B. Davis, "City Council Votes to Ban Medical Marijuana Dispensaries," *BeniciaPatch*, February 2, 2011. http://benicia.patch.com.
18. Quoted in Davis, "City Council Votes to Ban Medical Marijuana Dispensaries."
19. Drug Free America Foundation, "Marijuana."
20. Angel Raich, "Who Is Angel McClary Raich?," Angel's Fight to Stay Alive, 2010. www.angeljustice.org.
21. Quoted in Steven Portnoy, "White

House Drug Czar: Teen Marijuana Use on the Rise," ABC News, December 14, 2010. http://abcnews.go.com.

22. Quoted in Paul Armentano, "Drug Czar Blames Rising Teen Pot Use on Medical Cannabis Laws Rather than Gov't Failed Policies," *AlterNet*, December 17, 2010. http://blogs.alter net.org.

23. Dennis M. Gorman and J. Charles Huber Jr., "Do Medical Cannabis Laws Encourage Cannabis Use?" *International Journal of Drug Policy*, May 2007. www.ncbi.nlm.nih.gov.

Should Marijuana Be a Legal Substance?

24. Glenn Greenwald, *Drug Decriminalization in Portugal: Lessons for Creating Fair and Successful Drug Policies*. Washington, DC: Cato Institute, 2009, p. 1.

25. Greenwald, *Drug Decriminalization in Portugal*, p. 1.

26. Quoted in Kevin A. Sabet, "The Price of Legalizing Pot Is Too High," *Los Angeles Times*, June 7, 2009. http://articles.latimes.com.

27. Quoted in Sabet, "The Price of Legalizing Pot Is Too High."

28. Ronald Reagan, "Remarks on Signing Executive Order 12368, Concerning Federal Drug Abuse Policy Functions," Ronald Reagan Presidential Library, June 24, 1982. www.reagan.utexas.edu.

29. Ethan Nadelmann, "Marijuana Legalization: Not If, but When," *Huffington Post*, November 3, 2010. www.huffingtonpost.com.

30. Robert MacCoun and Peter Reuter, "Evaluating Alternative Cannabis Regimes," *British Journal of Psychiatry*, February 2001, p. 127. http://bjp.rcps ych.org.

31. State of California, "Proposition 19: Legalizes Marijuana Under California but Not Federal Law. Permits Local Governments to Regulate and Tax Commercial Production, Distribution, and Sale of Marijuana. Initiative Statute," Official Title and Summary, Prepared by the Attorney General. http://cdn.sos.ca.gov.

32. Beau Kilmer et al., "Altered State? Assessing How Marijuana Legalization in California Could Influence Marijuana Consumption and Public Budgets," occasional paper. Santa Monica, CA: RAND Drug Policy Research Center, 2010.

How Effective Are Efforts to Prevent Marijuana Use?

33. Ernest L. Abel, "Marijuana—the First Twelve Thousand Years," Schaffer Library of Drug Policy, 1990. www.druglibrary.org/Schaffer/hemp/his tory/first12000/12.htm.

34. Quoted in Tamala M. Edwards and Romesh Rathesar, "Lies, Tight Spots (and Other Near Death Experiences)," *Time*, August 31, 1998. www.time.com.

35. Quoted in Katharine Q. Seelye, "Barack Obama, Asked About Drug History, Admits He Inhaled," *New York Times*, October 24, 2006. www.nytimes.com.

36. Quoted in "Drug Policy Changes Under New Director," NPR, November 3, 2009. www.npr.org.

List of Illustrations

Is Marijuana a Dangerous Drug?
Evidence of Addiction   32
Marijuana Potency on the Rise   33
Marijuana as a Gateway Drug?   34

Should Marijuana Be Legal for Medical Use?
Strong Support for Medical Marijuana   47
Medical Marijuana Is Legal in 15 States   48

Should Marijuana Be a Legal Substance?
Support for Legalization Grows   62
The Decriminalization and Relaxation of Marijuana Laws   63
Marijuana Versus Alcohol   64

How Effective Are Efforts to Prevent Marijuana Use?
Changing Perception of Marijuana Risks   77
Parental Disapproval Plays a Role in Teen Marijuana Use   78
Teens Say Marijuana Is Easy to Get   79

Index

Note: Boldface page numbers indicate illustrations.

Above the Influence (National Youth Anti-Drug Media Campaign), 70
abuse victims, marijuana use by, 22
addictive potential
    arguments for, 6, 24–25, 28, 31, **32**
    arguments against, 7, 28, 71
    as gateway drug, 25–26, 29, 34, **34**
AIDS. See HIV/AIDS
Alaska, 47
Alcohol Drug Abuse Resource Center, 24–25
alcohol use/abuse
    deaths from, 28
    marijuana regulation compared with regulation of, 61, **64**
    marijuana use combined with
        increased rate of cancer, 24
        increased rate of car accidents, 56
        increased rate of violence, 21
    number of people seeking treatment for, **32**
    in substance abuse sequence, 25
    by teenagers, 77
American Journal of Psychiatry, 31
American Medical Association, 37
Americans for Safe Access, 84
Anslinger, Harry J., 11–12
Anti-Drug Abuse Act (1986), 52, 83
anxiety, 7, 22, 23, 35
Armentano, Paul, 44
athletes, use by, 66
Aunt Sandy's Medical Marijuana Cookbook (Moriarty), 38
auto accidents, 33, 34, 56
availability of marijuana, **79**

basal ganglia, 20
Benson, John A., Jr., 36
birth defects, disputed link between marijuana use and, 23
Black, David R., 73
blunt, 10
brain, effects on, 19–20, 28, 31
Burton, Robert, 82

California
    decriminalization in
        as ballot issue, 55–56
        increase in use and, 54
        for medical use, 17
        penalty for possession, 53
    early ban in, 11
    medical users in, as percentage of US total, 46
Canada, 12, 16
cancer
    marijuana as cause of, 19, 24
    marijuana as effective in relief of symptoms of, 36, 37, 43
cannabis, use of term, 9
Cannabis Eradication/Suppression Program, 67
Cannabis sativa, 9, **9**, 10
car accidents, associated with marijuana use, 33, 34, 56
Carter, Gregory T., 19
Central America, drug cartels in, 14
cerebellum, 20
chemical dependency, 24–25
children of users, effects on health of, 33

chronic pain, 37, 40–41
cigarette smoking, 24, 28
Clinton, Bill, 66
cocaine
    marijuana as gateway drug to, 25, 34, 62
    number of addicts seeking treatment, **32**
    supported by marijuana sales, 14
Cole, Jack, 59, 80
Common Sense for Drug Policy (CSDP), 84
consumption. See use of marijuana
Controlled Substances Act (1970), 12–13, 83
costs, of war on drugs, 52–53, 64
    legalization will decrease, 61, 64
        legalization will increase revenues to offset, 40, 54, 55, 59, 61
        to prison and court systems, 52
        to public health, 29
crime
    legalization will reduce, 53
    medical dispensaries and, 40
    use contributes to, 56
    violent, 21, 30
    See also law enforcement
cultivation in US, 13

deaths
    from alcohol and tobacco, 28
    decrease in Portugal with decriminalization, 51
    marijuana overdoses have not caused, 7, 28, 32
decriminalization
    international, 51–52, 59
    public opinion on, 61
    by states and District of Columbia
        effects of, 53–54
        for medical use, 7, 11, 16–17, 46, 47, **48**
Degenhardt, Louisa, 29
delivery methods
    edible products, 10, 38
    of Marinol, 38–39
    for medical use, 36, 40
    smoking, 10, 23, 36, 37
delta-9-tetrahydrocannabinol (THC). See THC (delta-9-tetrahydrocannabinol)
depression, 7, 22, 31
dispensaries for medical use, 40
Dixie, Dora, 43
Drug Abuse Warning Network (DAWN), 31
Drug Awareness Resistance Education (D.A.R.E.), 68–69
drug cartels, 14
drug courts, 68
Drug Free America Foundation, 38, 45, 80
Drug Free Communities, 70
Drug Policy Alliance (DPA), 80, 84
drug schedules, 12–13
drug testing, 70
drug tourism, 51
DuPont, Robert L., 80
    on current policies, 59
    on importance of reducing use, 65
    on medical marijuana, 36, 37

Earleywine, Mitch, 41, 80
economy
    effect of legalization on, 49, 54

tax revenues and money saved from legalization, 40, 54, 59, 61, 64
educational achievement, 21–22
education and prevention. *See* prevention programs
effects, physical/psychological, 6
  age of beginning of use and, 22, 31
  on behavior, 21–22, 33, 34, 56
  on brain, 19–20, 28, 31
  on education, 21–22
  on emotions, 10, 21
  on employment, 22
  on health, 14, 19, 33
  on mental health, 15, 22, 28–29, 31
  physical, 23–24
  of synthetic THC, 39
  unknown pharmacological, 35
Elders, Jocelyn, 36
emergency room visits, 31
emotions, effect on, 10, 21
employment and use, 22

federal prosecution, 17, 45
Fifth Amendment, 12
Florida, 76
food, 10, 20
Foundation for a Drug-Free World, 74, 84–85
Frisher, Martin, 29

gangs, 14
gateway drug, 25–26, 29, 34, **34**, 62
Giannasio, Charles V., 28
Gieringer, Dale, 19, 23
glaucoma patients, marijuana use by, 43
Goldberg, Raymond, 75
Green Aid (Medical Marijuana Legal Defense and Education Fund), 80
Greenwald, Glenn, 59
Grinspoon, Lester, 35, 44

Hall, Wayne, 29
Harrison Narcotics Act (1914), 82
hashish/hash, 10
health
  of children of users, 33
  costs, public, 29
  emergency room visits, 31
  negative effects on, 19, 22, 23–24
  positive effects on, 19, 22, 24
  public opinion about risks to, 6, 68, 69
  See also medical marijuana; mental health
hemp, 11
heroin
  marijuana as gateway drug to, 25, 34, 62
  number of addicts seeking treatment, 32
  as Schedule I drug, 12
  supported by marijuana sales, 14
hippocampus, 20
history of marijuana use, 10–13, 65–67, 71
HIV/AIDS
  spread of, 21
  use of marijuana to relieve symptoms of, 36, 37, 43, 46
Holder, Eric, 45
hormonal effects, 23
hunger, 20

importation, 13–14
Independent (magazine), 15
industry, value of, 49
infertility, disputed link between marijuana use and, 23

inhibitions, reduction of, 21
intelligence, effect on, 20, 28, 31
Investigational New Drug Compassionate Access Program (1978), 83

Jamestown, Virginia, 11
jazz, early association with marijuana use, 65–66
joint, 10
"Just Say No" antidrug campaign, 52

Kerlikowske, R. Gil, 81
  on harmful effects, 19
  on legalization, 41, 50, 59
  on prearrest diversion programs, 68
Koch, Ed, 50

LaGuardia Committee, 82
law enforcement
  alternatives to incarceration, 67–68
  arrests related to marijuana, 63
  cost of, 52–53, 64
  federal prosecution, 17, 45
  has failed, 57, 74
  has successfully cut supply, 67
  money saved from legalization, 56, 57, 61
Law Enforcement Against Prohibition (LEAP), 53, 81
laws
  federal/state, 11–13, 52–53, 76, 82, 83
  international, 51–52, 83
  See also specific acts
legalization
  arguments against, 18
    will increase burden on government regulation, 50, 58
    will increase use, 54, 58, 64
  arguments for
    recreational use is harmless, 17–18
    will decrease burden on law enforcement,
    will decrease cost of drug, 64
    will increase safety of marijuana, 56
    will increase tax revenues, 40, 54, 59, 61
    will not increase use, 54, 58
    will reduce crime, 53
    will save government resources, 17, 45, 50, 56, 57, 61
  as ballot issue, 55–56
  current policy is successful, 59
  decriminalization versus, **63**
  early, 11–13
  federal prosecution and, 17, 45
  is inevitable, 60
  in localities, 17
  for medical use
    in Canada, 16
    currently in states and District of Columbia, 7, 11, 16–17, 46, 47, **48**
    does increase recreational use, 45
    does not increase recreational use, 41
    job creation and, 49
    opposition of pharmaceutical companies, 39
    organized medicine opinion on, 41–42
    public opinion about, 7, 46, **47**, 48, **48**
    sends wrong message, 41
  public opinion, 7, 49, 54–55, 62, **62**
  status, 7
  view of government control over choices and, 60
  See also decriminalization
"Legalize It" (Tosh), 54
Levine, Jesse, 58
Lieberman, Jeffrey, 28

Life Skills Training, 69
limbic system, effect on, 21
Litwin, Craig, 40
Lloyd, Charlie, 27
local laws, 17
Louisiana, 76
LSD, as Schedule I drug, 12
Lynch, Tim, 74

Marijuana & Money (television program), 49
Marijuana Policy Project (MPP), 43, 81, 85
Marijuana Tax Act (1937), 11–12, 82
"Marijuana—the First Twelve Thousand Years" (Schaffer
    Library of Drug Policy), 66
Marinol, 38–39
Marley, Bob, 66
McKeganey, Neil, 27
medical marijuana, 7, **16**
    benefits of, 35–37, 40–41, 43
    delivery methods
        mouth spray, 83
        pill (Marinol), 39
        potential (inhaler/patch), 39
        smoking, 36, 37
    dispensaries, 40
    does not increase recreational use, 41, 45
    effectiveness of synthetic THC, 39
    federal prosecution of, 17, 45
    in history, 10, 82
    increases recreational use, 40, 45
    is harmful, 37, 39, 44
    legalization of
        in Canada, 16
        organized medicine opinion on, 41–42
        public opinion on, 7, 46, **47**, 48, **48**
        sends wrong message, 41
        in states and District of Columbia, 7, 11, 16–17,
            46, 47, **48**
    number of Americans in programs for, 46
    per patient average monthly usage, 49
    during pregnancy, 23
    public opinion on, 35–36, 46, **47**
    research on, 36, 37, 46
    unknown pharmacological effects of, 35
Medical Marijuana Information Resource Centre, 16
memory and learning impairment, 20
mental health, 22, 28–29, 31
methods of use. *See* delivery methods
Mexico, 12–13, 67
Michigan, 17
Montana, 47
mood, effect on, 21
multiple sclerosis, effects on symptoms of, 36, 37, 43
munchies, 20
musicians, use by, 54, 65–66

Nadelmann, Ethan, 53, 60
Narconon International, 74
Narcotics Control Act (1956), 12
National Center on Addiction and Substance Abuse, 85
National Institute on Drug Abuse (NIDA), 14–15, 21–22,
    28, 85
National Organization for the Reform of Marijuana Laws
    (NORML), 13, 28, 76, 81, 86
National Youth Anti-Drug Media Campaign, 70
nausea, prevention and treatment of, 7, 23, 35, 36, 37, 38,
    39
Nelson, Willie, 8, 54, 81
Netherlands, 51–52

neurons, 19–20
neurotransmitters, 20
Newsweek (magazine), 46
New York Times (newspaper), 12
1960s counterculture, 12

Obama, Barack, 66–67
Office of National Drug Control Policy (ONDCP), 86
    function of, 52
    on legalization, 58
    on medical use, 35
    on negative effects of use, 29
    prevention programs, 70
    on reducing use, 65
Ohio, 54
Oklahoma, 76
Oregon, 47, 49, 53
overdose, 7, 19, 28

pain relief
    alternatives to marijuana for, 43
    historical use of marijuana for, 10, 11
    marijuana is effective for, 7, 36, 37, 40–41, 46
    marijuana is safe for, 44
    neurotransmitters and, 20
parental influence on teenage marijuana use, **78**
Partnership at DrugFree.org, 74
Partnership for a Drug-Free America, 86
Phelps, Michael, 66
physical coordination impairment, 20
Portugal, 51–52, 59
potency, increase in, 6, 27, 31, **33**
pot parties, 12
prearrest diversion programs, 68
pregnancy, marijuana use during, 23
prevention programs
    are effective, 73, 74
    are not effective, 18, 73, 74, 75, 76
    community based, 70, 74
    fact-based, 74
    importance of drug testing, 70
    "Just Say No" campaign, 52
    media campaigns, 69–70
    peer, 73
    public opinion on, 7, 76
    risk perception and, 68, **77**
    scare tactic approach, 74
    school-based, 68–69
prison sentences, mandatory, 52
Project ALERT, 69
Project Deliverance, 67
Proposition 19 (California), 55–56
psychoactive ingredients, 9–10
public opinion
    on addicts, 30
    on availability of marijuana, **79**
    on costs of law enforcement, 64
    on decriminalization, 61
    on health risks, 6, 68, 69
    on legalization, 7, 54–55, 62, **62**
        effect on economy, 49
        for medical use, 7, 46, **47**, 48, **48**
    on marijuana as gateway drug, 62
    on medical use, 35–36, 46, **47**
    on prevention programs, 7, 76
    on risks to health, 6, 68, 69, **77**
    on taxation/regulation, 64
    in Portugal, 51

Raich, Angel, 40–41, 81
Reagan, Ronald, 52
recreational use
    banned, 11
    decriminalization of, 51–52, 53–54
    is increased by allowing medical use, 40, 45
    is not increased by allowing medical use, 41
Reefer Madness (1936 film), 11, 82
reggae, 66
Regulate, Control and Tax Cannabis Act (California, 2010),
    55–56
Reist, Dan, 73, 75
religious uses, 11
research
    on children of users, 33
    on decriminalization, 54
    on harmful health effects, 19, 24
    limitations on, 36
    on medical use, 37, 46
Room, Robin, 29

Sativex, 38
Schedule I drugs, 12
schizophrenia, 22, 28
Schwarzenegger, Arnold, 53
serotonin, 20
sexual behavior, 21
skunk/skunk weed, 6, 21
smoking marijuana
    dangers of, 23, 24, 36, 37
    history of, 10
smoking tobacco products, 24, 28
sources of marijuana, 13–14
South America, drug cartels in, 14
Southwest Border Counternarcotics Strategy, 67
Stamper, Norm, 8
states
    laws against possession
        alternatives to incarceration, 67–68
        earliest, 11
        toughest, 76
        zero tolerance, 52
    legalization for medical use in, 16–17, **48**
        limits on amounts possessed, 47
        number of, 7, 26
        population of, 61
    primary, for cultivation, 13
    revenue from legalization, 54
stimulants, teens seeking treatment for addiction to, **32**
StoptheDrugWar.org, 81
Substance Abuse and Mental Health Services Administration
    (SAMHSA), 30, 56, 87
substance abuse sequence, 25
supply chain
    described, 14
    grown in US, 76
    efforts to stop/disrupt
        DEA seizure of traffickers' assets, 52
        have been successful, 67
        have not been successful, 18, 67, 74, 76, **79**
Supreme Court cases, 12, 83
synthetic THC, 38–39

Tashkin, Donald, 24
teenagers
    availability of marijuana to, 18, 76, **79**
    effects of marijuana use on
        addiction and age at first use, 34
        education, 21–22

    hormonal vulnerabilities and, 23
    mental illness and age at first use, 22
    schizophrenia risk, 28
    prearrest diversion programs for, 68
    smoking skunk by, 15
    use by
        average daily, of alcohol and drugs, 77
        decrease in, 41
        parental influence on, 78, **78**
    See also gateway drug
THC (delta-9-tetrahydrocannabinol), 9, 83
    car accidents and, 56
    duration in human system of, 20
    effects of
        on behavior, 21–22
        on brain, 19–20
        on emotions, 10
    increase in percentage of, 31
    pathway of, 10
    synthetic, 38–39
Tindall, Judith A., 73
Tosh, Peter, 54
traffickers. *See* supply chain
treatment
    number of teens seeking, **32**
    programs, 70–72
    public knowledge as deterrent to, 79
    withdrawal symptoms and, 25, 72

United Nations Office on Drugs and Crime, 27
US Department of Justice, 17, 45
US Drug Enforcement Administration (DEA), 87
    efforts to stop supply, 67
    on Marinol, 39
    seizure of traffickers' assets, 52
    on source of marijuana, 13
    on supply chain, 13, 14
use of marijuana
    age of first, 22, 31, 34
    contributes to crime, 56
    decriminalization of, 53–54
    delivery methods
        edible products, 38
        of Marinol, 38–39
        for medical use, 36, 40
        smoking, 10, 23, 36, 37
    efforts to reduce, 67, 68–70
    prevalence of, 6, 8, 76
    recreational
        banned, 11
        decriminalization of, 51–52, 53–54
        is increased by allowing medical use, 40, 45
        is not increased by allowing medical use, 41
    religious, 11
    by teenagers
        average daily, 77
        decrease in, 41
        opinion about risk and, **77**
        parental influence on, 78, **78**
    See also medical use
US Food and Drug Administration (FDA), 38

violence, associated with marijuana use, 21, 30, 82

Waldock, Katherine, 60
Williams, Ricky, 66
withdrawal symptoms, 25, 72
Woodstock, New York, music festival, 12